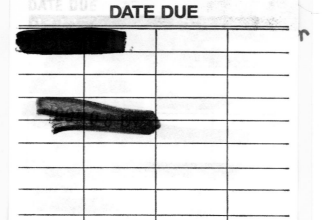

GW

Defoe and the Uses of Narrative

DEFOE

and

the Uses of Narrative

Michael M. Boardman

Rutgers University Press
New Brunswick, New Jersey

*Publication of this book has been aided by a grant
from the National Endowment for the Humanities.*

Library of Congress Cataloging in Publication Data

Boardman, Michael M., 1945–
  Defoe and the uses of narrative.

  Bibliography: p.
  Includes index.
  1. Defoe, Daniel, 1661?–1731—Criticism and
interpretation.   2. Narration (Rhetoric).   I. Title.
PR3407.B6   823'.5   82-3652
ISBN 0-8135-0961-0   AACR2

For Jean Sacks,
in Memory of
Sheldon Sacks

Contents

Preface

FOR ANYONE CONCERNED, as I am, with the objective bases of literary experience, Defoe presents serious difficulties. In tracing a theory of formal development through Richardson, Fielding, or Jane Austen, we can with some confidence depend on our texts to determine some fundamental meanings. Although these later novelists fall victim to their own brands of narrative disjunction, their intention was to write coherent, overtly fictional, strongly patterned novels. Since unity has the effect of producing a sort of "community of values," for at least the story's duration, we need not anticipate profound disagreement about whether, say, Fielding intends Parson Adams or Tom to be admirable. Rigorous assertion that Anne Elliot deserves her final happiness or that Emma's character changes in an important way would be unnecessary, even noisome, iterations of the obvious.

Discussions of Defoe, by contrast, have from the beginning been marked by radical disagreement about matters that have become almost critical commonplaces with the later novelists. What is *Robinson Crusoe* about? Is Moll admirable and her repentance sincere? Is Roxana some sort of fiend, or some sort of tragic heroine? Faced with such "simple" questions and interested in the larger issue of narrative development, I was forced to consider the possibility that

Defoe did not customarily achieve systematic yoking of his materials to single unifying intentions, not even to the extent that inconsistencies could be seen as "violations" of even a frail coherence. Perhaps a hypothesis of multiple, fluctuating narrative use might explain my intuitive apprehension, which I found shared by other readers, that Defoe seemed frequently to be testing out a variety of ways of ordering and giving significance to narrative experience.

With such a thesis, one procedure I scrupulously had to avoid was the imposition, by any means, of overarching schemes of unity. I began to suspect that the confidently communicating artist some had found in Defoe was largely a critical fiction, a product of a kind of criticism that never fails to find coherence precisely because of how coherence has initially been defined. I was interested in no favorite dialectical construct, no convenient "code," in recent parlance. If my impression of Defoe as a tentative explorer was correct, a matter-of-fact method might reveal more about Defoe's struggles, his sometimes tentative sorties into narrative unknown territory, than a method that created the unity it could not find.

It may therefore appear to many readers that I have ruled out more questions, and more interesting ones, than I have answered. Yet this is always the spectacle of criticism. We get what we bargain for, and what I wanted was an understanding of Defoe's manipulations of subjects and techniques, the implied effects on readers, and his place, given those questions, in the history of narrative. My underlying assumption was, and is, that writing poems or novels is a special kind of "making," a "task," as T. S. Eliot put it, "in the same sense as the making of an efficient engine or the turning of a jug or a table-leg," a view he shared with, of course, Aristotle. My quarrels with earlier critics, who have admirably pursued other lines of inquiry, should be understood in this light.

I am grateful to the National Endowment for the Humanities for a grant that started me on this project, and to my wife, Betty, for the encouragement that kept me going. For Teresa Toulouse and Philip Bollier special thanks are in order for their sensitive criticism of portions of the typescript. Gwin J. Kolb's advice and friendship have been invaluable, and my debt to Ralph W. Rader, apparent throughout, is matched only by my gratitude for his assistance.

Finally, this book is dedicated to Sheldon Sacks and his wife, Jean, in memory of his humane insight and friendship and in thanks for her continuing affection and regard.

I
Defoe and Narrative Traditions

DEFOE WROTE AT A TIME when many literary conventions must have seemed exhausted. The great Christian epic had finally appeared, and few wished seriously to contest for Milton's crown. English drama in Defoe's time seems constantly to try to better Shakespeare, improve his plays, or to invent types, like the heroic play, earlier dramatists had not essayed. In general, their attempts to exorcise the Elizabethan ghosts fall short of complete success. Poetry had already turned away from the lyric and personal and toward what Boswell later in the century would call the "ethick." The poem was now often a vehicle for argument eloquently embellished, for exemplifying in verse "What oft was thought, but ne'er so well expressed." Similar pressures for change were bearing on prose narrative, which entailed in its use other limitations, inherited from a tradition of pragmatic use. Narrative that merely told a story, for the story's own sake, was frivolous; we can catch the condescension in Johnson's voice as he describes "heroic romance": "almost all the fictions of the last age will vanish, if you deprive them of a hermit and a wood, a battle and a shipwreck."[1] Legitimate use of fictional narrative was limited to clearly didactic allegory, like Bunyan's, or satire, such as Baldwin's *Beware the Cat*, or the anonymous *Lazarillo de Tormes*, with the aim being to benefit and amuse even the rudely learned. Fiction remained "low"; the respectable use of narrative was in history, in all its guises. If an author wished to fabulate in narrative, and rejected the satiric and didactic impulses, he had to cloak his artistry, conceal his creative presence behind a mask of literal verisimilitude. For the born storyteller, French or English, prose was neither socially nor artistically attractive.

Defoe's career, from the early 1700s, therefore reveals a man searching for viable narrative strategies that tradition and convention had denied him or had withdrawn from the public repertoire. Dozens of Defoe's hundreds of works are narratives. Few of them are easy to describe. They lack single principles of being, fit no prescriptive categories, in part because Defoe is creating the possibilities for narrative as he goes along. Most of Defoe's stories, before *Robinson Crusoe*, are amalgams of intention and effect, requiring us to look very closely at how they fluctuate through time in order to understand them. He seldom wrote, for example, unmixed and easily recognizable irony—although he was capable of it—preferring instead to hide his intention behind opaque impersonation or overpower his enemies with invective, unable to decide whether to "rally" or "rail" at his readers.[2] He loved history, and loved to deflect historical narrative to purposes not specifically historical, for example, to justifying or discrediting a political cause. He liked to insert brief stories into his moralistic works, so that his readers could receive their "medicine of cherries." Wherever we look, even long before *Robinson Crusoe*, Defoe is experimenting with the materials, the techniques, the language, and the possible effects of stories.

What Defoe does to accept or rebel against the constraints of a limited narrative tradition is therefore a matter of some importance, especially since the nature of narrative has become one of the most debated critical problems today. What is now needed is a better understanding of just what resources and possible uses of narrative were available to Defoe when he began, with *Robinson Crusoe*, and how he modified some things he found and left others unchanged. We have evidence from a variety of sources that some important transformations were taking place in narrative in the eighteenth century. Not only have many critics dated the novel from then, but Fielding and Richardson, different as they were, also thought they were doing something new; and Johnson, in the *Rambler* essay on fiction to which I have already referred, says that the "task of our present writers is very different"—from the writers of romance, that is. Until recently, few would have had any difficulty accepting the notion of a traditional novel. Even Robbe-Grillet needs the concept with which to contrast his nouveau roman. The other question, where Defoe comes from, is more problematical, but not insoluble, unless we approach it with a prior assumption that the complexities of a Defoe can be explained as the product of a single tradition or the result of a single strategy.

My general question really involves, then, both poetics and criticism. Precisely how narrative transformations come about, why they occur, and what they entail for reader response and meaning compose one set of questions. Yet those cannot be answered in isolation from particular texts. One must work toward understanding the synchronic paradigm of Defoe's narrative career in order to grasp the dynamics of the diachronic development of the novel and other related narrative types. The method I propose is dialectical, using Defoe's works as an achieved body of potentialities and actualities to illuminate the transformation, through time, of narrative forms, while allowing the larger question to make possible our view of Defoe himself. I shall begin with the second and by no means simpler problem, Defoe's development.

Homogeneity or Mutation?

Between 1719 and 1724, Defoe wrote the eight major narratives on which his reputation rests today. Read in chronological order, as best it can be determined, they tend to abide in the memory as a kind of seamless fabric, marked by no radical departures from their own routines of presentation. In each, a first-person narrator recounts his or her life, in episodes usually reaching back into childhood, and in simple and direct language as countersensational as the events are bizarre. To call them novels begs the question these books pose. The illusion, a stubborn one, is that Crusoe, Moll, Jack, and all the rest are telling their own stories, mediated, if at all, only by the bowdlerizing exertions of a shadowy editor. Variations there are, of course. From Crusoe to Roxana, the materials of story vary widely: seafaring, soldiering, stealing, whoring; desert islands and pestiferous cities; wealth, poverty, and the middle state Defoe believed most conducive to virtuous ease. Sometimes he seems intent on external events, sometimes on the fluctuations of his narrators' psyches, and sometimes on a kind of fascinating interaction between world and mind. Yet the similarities of these works, in their modes of progression, in their subdued presentation of wondrous occurrences, in the very rhythms of their discourse, have made any differences seem less important. It is not really surprising then that critics have usually taken a panoramic view of Defoe. Whether calling these odd performances novels, or protonovels, or denying them, as Ralph Rader does, entry into the house of the traditional novel, Defoe's venerators and detractors alike, with few exceptions, have decided that he knew but a single way of telling a story. As Sir Leslie Stephen long ago said, Defoe had "only one mode . . . a good steady jog-trot of narrative."[3] More recently, Alan D. McKillop explicitly stated the case against seeing any sort of artful progression. Defoe simply "proceeded by trial and error." It is, McKillop argues, "impossible to arrange" Defoe's narratives "in a sequence that will clearly show development by artistic self-discovery." It is only McKillop's qualifying "clearly," I shall try to show, that makes him correct, by definition, since Defoe's development is not easily perceived. Even so, McKillop immediately goes on to say that Defoe "seems to be moving in several directions at once, to be reverting to old ways as well as to be advancing and experimenting."[4] Other dismissals seem less fundamental but raise other important questions about the explanatory force of some of our developmental theories. David Goldknopf, for example, denies Defoe "progressive emancipation from the conven-

4

tion of reportage" because Defoe, in his last narrative, "insists that Roxana's story is true."[5] Clearly, however, Defoe's prefatory asseveration of the literal truth of a story does not necessarily require him to write a story itself exhibiting a configuration of truth, a confirmatory illusion matching the authorial pose. Indeed, we shall see that Defoe, like many writers, does not fully understand at all times what he is doing or, because of his assumptions about the uses of narrative, does not report his intentions accurately.

The central problem of Defoe studies is not, however, determining what he *thought* he was doing. It is, rather, that critics have employed methods that virtually ensure they will see Defoe's narratives as a solid and essentially unvarying whole. Ian Watt, in his discussion of *Moll Flanders*, contends that "most of what is said here . . . of Defoe's treatment of plot, character, and total literary structure, holds good for all his novels." In fairness, it must be granted that Watt's thesis demands that he find, as a common denominator, formal realism uniting not only all of Defoe but other examples of the "rise of the novel."[6] Even so, from Sir Leslie Stephen to one of the more recent critics of Defoe, Everett Zimmerman, the unanimous and ineluctable verdict has been that Defoe exhibits the "same" basic "achievement from *Robinson Crusoe* to *Roxana*."[7]

Yet, if one construes the facts of Defoe's career differently, this homogeneity disappears. In a moment, I shall suggest why Defoe's development has remained hidden from so many perspicacious critics. For now, it is enough to say that I claim no grand things for him, no arrival at some majestic apotheosis of novelistic form. He is indeed important to the innovation of what came to be known as the traditional novel, but he always clung tenaciously to the older historical and pseudohistorical traditions from which his works rose and from which they drew sustenance. He wrote no single narrative that can satisfactorily be analyzed as a coherent novel and his century recognized the fact. As McKillop notes, Defoe's narratives stirred "no critical excitement about the appearance of a 'new way' or 'new species' of writing."[8] Richardson and Fielding do not even acknowledge him as a distant, unlettered, somewhat embarrassing cousin, much less commemorate him as paterfamilias. In part, the neglect of Defoe in his own century stems from ignorance: readers associated him with *Robinson Crusoe*, of course, but primarily they thought of Defoe as the man who had written *The Shortest Way with the Dissenters* and had been pilloried for his impudence. Even had his century known what he had written, it is doubtful he would have been seen as doing anything particularly new. He starts and stops, transforms only to abandon, innovates toward dead ends; his artistic fitfulness obscures the figure in the carpet that emerges, finally, as a clear and important pattern of narrative experimentation.

Beginning with *Robinson Crusoe*, which contains all the potentialities for what he would later do, Defoe moves in two fundamentally different courses. He gradually develops the subjects, techniques, and potential effects of narrative that not only purports to be true but carries with it an illusion of truth so opaque as to be impenetrable. He writes fiction, like the *Journal of the Plague Year*, that stubbornly insists, if one is to make full sense of it, that one forgets it is fiction. At the same time, he experiments with ways of subverting his own illusory structures, of including within an overall illusion of historicity the knowledge that the reader is participating in a basically fictional world. He stumbles upon fictional situations, tries to dispense with them, only to have his own imagination betray him. This second line, this grudging fabulation, leads directly to the innovation that is *Roxana*. Only there does Defoe evolve anything like the authorial psychology or create the teleology and effect of the novel yet to be born; and even in *Roxana*, the enterprise produces a novel *manqué*. He ceases writing major fiction in 1724—fulfilled, frustrated, or merely spent—leaving the field to the next generation of storytellers.

For some, my attempt to determine where Defoe fits into the history of the novel will simply be naive. As Scholes and Kellogg taught us, many of the strategies the novel enacts were present in earlier narrative.[9] But that is not my question. For two hundred years, many historians and critics have felt that narrative in England did change during the first half of the eighteenth century, whether 1719 or 1740 is chosen as the signal year. Surely the question retains some viability, if only for our understanding of how we have gone about classifying literary events in the past. The problem is in part metacritical, in part historical: the genesis of the novel was a reality in England and Defoe's place in that genesis important but misunderstood. Even so, I am left with a difficulty only partly rhetorical. No one, I suppose, would automatically consign me to the ranks of the critically benighted if I suggested Defoe was not a traditional novelist; but neither would I be accused of originality, since Rader has said as much. Similarly, to argue, on perhaps some basis as yet unheard of, that Defoe was instead the first modern novelist would be neither new nor particularly venturesome. What I propose as an alternative, in an act of seemingly timid irresolution, is that Defoe was neither the first figure on the novel's horizon nor the last practitioner of a fading tradition, lying like the truth. Neither capstone nor foundation, Defoe's role was transitional. He writes at a time when narrative must find new employment. One must therefore understand not only his structures, but also his stories' functions and modes of communication—to use Wolfgang Iser's concepts—in order to grasp his meaning and his place in literary history.[10] If he fails, even in *Roxana*, his swan song, to achieve anything like a novelistic whole, his exertions still tell a fascinating story about the difficulty of narrative innovation. That story is my subject. But first, at the necessary risk of appearing contentious, it may be useful to explain why Defoe's career has not been fully understood.

The Ideological Imperative and an Alternative

The tendency to see Defoe's narratives as one thing may be traced to two sources. Apart from the similarities of presentation that seem to unite these eight books, Defoe argued for most of them a didactic intention. In his justification for giving the public these stories, he echoes Horace, Cicero, Sidney, and countless other rhetoricians and critics, English and Continental, ancient and modern, who counseled finding the moral and then constructing an appropriate fable to carry it. Defoe plainly invites his readers to "make good Uses" of the story, to be "more pleased with the Moral, than the Fable, with the Application than the Relation."[11] Nineteenth-century critics were dubious about the application and appalled by the relation, at least in such works as *Moll Flanders* and *Roxana*. Our century has, by and large, taken Defoe at his word and set out to codify the meaning he said would be found. Indeed, significance of some sort is the central goal of most recent novel criticism, not only of Defoe but of the novel as a genre. How does narrative mean? J. Paul Hunter is just one example of a critic who finds *Robinson Crusoe* to be an advance over previous travel adventures because the latter "seem to lack ideological content, and no thematic meaning can be abstracted from them."[12] Now, this statement is a bit misleading, since, if desired, one can tease meaning from anything, including Sterne's inky page.[13] But Hunter's assumptions about how to understand Defoe are widely shared and indeed have led to most of the insights that have been gained into Defoe the past few years. Maximillian E. Novak's method was to "establish Defoe's general opinions on natural law and human nature as they appear in his didactic works and . . . proceed to a detailed examination of his fiction, showing how these ideas manifested themselves." George Starr looks for "the leading religious ideas in Defoe's fiction" and finds them to be "commonplaces of the English Protestant tradition." Watt, although he explores the technical accomplishment of *Moll Flanders* more rigorously than do these others, still asserts that "all Defoe's novels are . . . ethically neutral" because Defoe's obsessive interest in formal realism for its own sake precludes any "ulterior significance." Defoe fails for Watt, that is, on precisely the same grounds Defoe succeeds with other critics: semantic complexity. Faced with an allegorical interpretation of *Robinson Crusoe*, E. M. W. Tillyard seems a bit uneasy, remarking that "we have to decide whether to push such multiple significances farther." His answer: "Present fashion tempts us to push them much farther."

So he wrote in 1958. Someone had already managed to fulfill the prophecy: for one critic, Crusoe's success in making an earthen pot equates with "ultimate success in attaining a spiritual goal. . . . In a sense Crusoe is the pot himself."[14]

There can be no doubt that these books are fascinatingly *about* important issues. Defoe's concerns about man's place in a greedy and selfish society, his relationship with his God, his very nature as human animal, tempted by the Devil and swayed by necessity, depending on the fragile powers of reason to secure comfort the world would deny—emphatically these issues are there, on the page. The critics, such as Watt, Starr, Hunter, and so many others who have so well defined Defoe's topics, did not invent them. Their critical task has been to extrapolate from the "blooming, buzzing chaos" of Defoe's fictional world some order and pattern. The history of criticism should teach us that an abiding, and indubitably valid, approach to any author is to treat his thought as central. Taking fiction as a special kind of discourse continues to be not only a favorite procedure but virtually a fundamental assumption of many critics. Yet, as widespread as the semantic method is, it too has its liabilities; indeed, any "framework" excludes much more than it brings in. The difficulty with much earlier criticism of Defoe is that it has actually discouraged critics from even asking whether Defoe moved in various directions, apart from subject matter. It is as if, having in advance defined the essence of the novel as extractable meaning, and being able, by virtue of the potential allusiveness of words, to extract meaning from any stretch of language, critics have virtually guaranteed that Defoe will be a novelist, only because his stories can be made to signify. Their definition of the form, it might be said, proceeds from their favorite way of working. The same circularity may apply to anything one says about a text. But to define "novel" as thematic meaning, at least with Defoe, is to limit severely his role in the creation of new fictional forms, as well as to obscure his own development, which lies in other directions. In the quest for ideas, we may, as John Richetti recently remarked, have forgotten that discursive

9

statement differs, or can differ, in *kind* from fiction.[15] Although Watt seemed interested in the question of whether one can ever determine Defoe's meaning in *Moll Flanders*, he assumes that the rest of Defoe means, or fails to mean, in the same way Moll's story does. No one has yet started with the question of whether Defoe attempted to discover new ways to tell a story; if he did, his discoveries may very well entail different ways in which story can signify.

As far as development is concerned, therefore, single-variable schemes do not help one see whither goest Defoe. If, for example, technique alone is examined, one may be forced to conclude, as does an anonymous critic, that "all Defoe's novels . . . are but a string of separate anecdotes related by one person." Yet even this critic suspected that something more important was involved: "In no one of them are there forces at work that necessitate the conclusion of the story at a certain point."[16] Such forces, which are present in *Roxana*, would involve not only technique—order, point of view, episodic linkage—but language, subject matter, even the implied intent and effect. As long ago as Walter Wilson, it was known that something about Defoe frees readers to admire or dislike him "according to the bent of their tastes and opinions," in a way that the formal constraints of a Fielding or Austen do not easily permit. If it is true that we "must use our own insight and judgment if we wish to know what really was the interior character of Moll Flanders," then formal considerations alone would never be adequate to determining the nature and effect of these books.[17] We would have to understand both the mind of their creator—what we could infer about it—and their "rhetoric," the ways in which they intrude into our minds, the mental operations they demand or permit. Questions about Defoe tend, in this way, to become cannibalistic.

To understand Defoe's development, therefore, one must go beyond mere subject, mere language, mere anything. One does not, I suggest, gain much by hearing that "*Robinson Crusoe* is certainly the first novel in the sense that it is the first fictional narrative in which an ordinary person's daily activities are the centre of continuous literary attention."[18] What does "ordinary" mean? Seventeenth-century narrative is full of figures who, despite their status, seem unremarkable enough. Is stripping the hero or heroine of wealth and power all the novel needed to be born? As a generic criterion, subject matter affords little explanatory power. One can proliferate connections; but what is gained by seeing *Robinson Crusoe* as the grandfather of *The Last Man* and the great-uncle of *Typee*? Once in awhile, critics have seen that the material of fiction is not the only determinant of effect. Arthur W. Secord perhaps put it best when he noted that "even in the Carleton story"—one of Defoe's most opaquely factual—"there are traces of an effort to manipulate the incidents for the artistic purposes of fiction."[19] Although far more suggestive than explanatory, Secord was one of the few critics who recognized that one must understand the process of Defoe's narratives, how they come into being, operate, and affect the reader, to say what they are.

A second general problem has been the tendency to see Defoe, and indeed all novelists, as essentially autobiographers of their own secret selves, a notion so common that it suggests Mill's "deep slumber of a decided opinion."[20] Scholes and Kellogg give one enunciation of the idea: "It is the novelists who tend to put themselves into their characters. . . . Is there not much of Defoe not only in Robinson Crusoe but in Moll Flanders and Roxana as well?" The general assumption is so widespread that critics do not even bother to produce evidence for the connection.[21] At work seems again to be something like what goes on with those who unify Defoe with schemes of semantic content. Since ideas Defoe expressed elsewhere appear in his fictions too, and since all of Defoe's figures appear to share certain similarities of character, Defoe *must* be lurking just behind them. Aside from managing again to fuse all of Defoe's narratives, this theory has some other unpleasant liabilities. It smacks, first, of a common recent reductive theory of behavior: if no obvious cause of some human activity presents itself, the cause must be hidden, buried in the muck of the subconscious. Since critics have had difficulty determining what Defoe's use of Moll really is, it is tempting to argue that he is working out on paper forbidden fantasies. Stodgy old Defoe, I admit, immediately gains new interest by acquiring a heady dose of latent lasciviousness. The problem, for a more literal-minded critic, is that it is hard to psychoanalyze a man dead for over two centuries, and, more fundamentally, there is plenty of evidence in Defoe and elsewhere, if we know what to look for, that authors do not always project their personalities with such rampant and distasteful indecorum. Even Virginia Woolf strove "to be released from the cramp and confinement of personality." Wayne Booth has warned that one must not automatically identify narrators with their creators.[22] This question must be treated later, because, like development, it is not a single issue. For now, it may be useful to entertain the notion that Defoe had no single relationship to his stories, any more than he had only one kind of story.

Traditions of Factuality

Development implies a beginning and a movement to something different. Influence need not, of course, always be external. Once Defoe wrote *Robinson Crusoe*, he had a model on which to work changes. Yet earlier traditions clearly played some part in delimiting a range of potentialities Defoe might pursue. Almost every kind of earlier narrative has risen as a candidate for the example on which Defoe patterned his great mythic tale. What should by now be obvious is that no single narrative tradition explains how Defoe came, at the age of fifty-nine or sixty, to write *Robinson Crusoe*. Much less do single traditions account for Defoe's intuition of the form his work should assume, its manifestation, and readers' continuing fascination with the book. Indeed, the dynamic relationship among author, work, and reader—the book as phenomenon—has gone largely unexamined, critics preferring instead to single out some aspect of subject matter from an older tradition and treat it as generative. J. Paul Hunter is not amiss, therefore, in arguing that Secord overemphasizes the influence of voyage literature, since "*Robinson Crusoe* makes no attempt to follow the conventional pattern of the travel tradition."[23] Even so, Starr's and Hunter's own attempts to assimilate the book to spiritual literature end up substituting another explanatorily inadequate paradigm, religion, for Secord's travel adventure. In fact, Secord's analyses are sometimes more flexible than these later critics', since he often considers not only subject but technique, language, and implied effect. Both ways of proceeding lead to important insights, but Hunter's desire to demonstrate that "Defoe's art" is "idea-centered" rather than "fact-centered"—since, if it were not, Defoe would not be a novelist according to Hunter's implicit definition—often leads him to value Defoe for the single attraction of ideas Hunter admits are commonplaces of the age. Such a method seeks, by intention, to confer homogeneity on chaos. Yet the history-of-ideas approach has led to precious little agreement about Defoe. Watt, for example, asks of *Robinson Crusoe*, as does Hunter, What does the book mean? but he concludes that "although religious concerns are present they have no . . . priority of status," the "heritage of Puritanism" being "too weak to supply a continuous and controlling pattern for the hero's experience." Watt then proffers his solution, and he too singles out a relatively small part of the book and finds it explanatory of the whole: Crusoe is *homo economicus* and "profit" is his "only vocation."[24] While Defoe does portray such concerns, the partial nature of them, as explanations, is obvious. Moreover, they do not really account for structure, much less genesis.

It may seem that I hold up unreasonable expectations for Defoe criticism. Of course, no single explanation ever exhausts the rich multiplicity of a text. The doctrine of pluralism states that any work can yield equally valid but necessarily incommensurable insights depending on the conceptual framework employed. This is not, as Iser recently suggested, relativism, since pluralism implies a matching of question and method not at all accidental.[25] The other side of the coin, however, is that all critical approaches preclude some insights as rigorously as they make others possible. Everything depends on what one desires to know. In the case of development, any method that restricts inquiry to a single source of narrative effects, or tends to coalesce what in another framework might seem significant differences, tends to make Defoe's development more difficult to perceive. As Martin Price suggests, "Defoe draws upon forms of autobiography as far apart as criminals' sensational narratives of their careers and Puritan preachers' records of their transactions with God and the devil, factual narratives of sea discoveries, and pious accounts of miraculous providences."[26] Of course, this is what Defoe did, but these varieties of narrative still serve only as potentialities, and no one of them explains *Robinson Crusoe*. If Defoe merely redacted parts of such works—a little adventure, a little spirituality—his narratives would indeed be the string of disjointed episodes some nineteenth-century critics said they were. By now, the scene of Defoe's activity may be fairly well understood, but little is known about the act, for which the choice of methods is responsible, a decision that always excludes something. For a change, one must look at the generic principles of Defoe's sources as well as their content.

With the exception of the picaresque—which has, in its classical Spanish examples, a satirical purpose that Defoe's narratives do not—and Bunyanesque fable—whose allegorical method and formulable meaning Defoe eschewed—all of the traditions suggested as candidates for influence share a factual or pseudofactual intention. They are varieties of history, veracious or illusory. Despite their obviously dissimilar subjects, they also share numerous conventions of technique and narrational stance, the created rhetorical relationship between author and reader that much more powerfully than subject defines narrative experience. Defoe had available, that is, not only a body of conventions and narrative *topoi*—the castaway, the orphan making her way in the world, the penitent sinner, and so forth—to draw upon and modify to his own purposes, but also a set of techniques. The basis for Defoe's experimentation was no single tradition, nor even the conventions of one tradition, but the possibilities inherent in a large number of factual and pseudofactual forms. He sought, not to replicate any single previous type, but to refine and epitomize many of the pleasurable and meaningful features of the multiplicitous literature of fact. The remaining chapters will show

how such a refining intention led him to his best effects and how he finally almost succeeded in breaking with these antecedents. For now, it is necessary to see how such a body of potentialities looked to Defoe as he began *Robinson Crusoe.*

Defoe was thoroughly familiar with the literature of fact. He once said, "truly I have read all the histories of Europe, that are extant in our language, and some in other languages." Yet, despite Defoe's confidence in his historical expertise, the documents from which he would have acquired it were treacherous. Anything that even purported to deal with actual people and events could have been considered history. Yet, probably at no other time have there existed so many memoirs, autobiographies, and "true accounts" that in reality were fabrications. Defoe refers, for example, to "the *Count de Rochefort's Memoirs,*" translated into English in 1696. Defoe quotes the book and expects his readers to know about it.[27] What Defoe apparently did not know was that Rochefort's "memoirs" came to him courtesy of a master French fabricator, Courtilz de Sandras. Courtilz, and others such as Hamilton, Préchac, and Dufossé, not to mention the ubiquitous Madame D'Aulnoy, all wrote personal memoirs of public figures who, lamentably but not irremediably, had failed to set down the details of their own lives. The relevance of such works, and of other traditions founded on the verisimilar lie, will appear when we see how Defoe adapted many of their strategies of internal confirmation to his own works. Paradoxically, then, Defoe borrows the techniques of history from works that are deceptions and uses those strategies for his own illusory purposes.

What Defoe would have seen in *Rochefort* and other pseudofactual works was not so much a subject for copying as a successful set of practices that would guarantee his books an air of truth. He would have learned, for example, that incredible pains must be taken with the mechanics of an illusion from a book like *The Memoires of the Dutchess Mazarine* (trans. 1676), sometimes attributed to the Abbé St. Real. The narrator frequently avers that she is trying to correct mistaken beliefs about her conduct. To cap the illusion, an "editor" appends a final letter, "containing a True Character of her Person and

Conversation" from someone who has read the memoirs in manu-
script and now returns them with his confirmation of their accuracy.
He adds a last little verifying touch: since the *Memoires* were written,
the Dutchess is sadly "altered." Everywhere one looks in late seventeenth-century narrative one finds real people acting, thinking, and
speaking realistically. The significant difference between these twi-
light performances and Defoe's imagined real people is no mere
formal realism, and, if this is true, much of Watt's thesis becomes
doubtful. Courtilz and Defoe both attempt to pass fiction off for
truth. Defoe's innovations lie, not only in endowing such tired old
illusions with emotional force, but also in the ways he finds to subvert
the illusion, at least in one line of his development.

Defoe begins, then, with an intention to deceive. It is, of course,
pleasurable, even significant deception. Probably no such thing as a
single factual *form* exists and, as McKillop remarks, "there is not
much point in sorting out Defoe's narrative details as true or
invented."[28] Yet Defoe's attempt to cloak fiction in the guise of truth
is important because it commits him to strategies of storytelling with
which he finally becomes uncomfortable. The fabulator who hides
traces of his activity, as he must if the illusion is to succeed, gains his
end only at the cost of closing off certain kinds of willed meaning and
experience. Defoe cannot, as Fielding can, claim credit for his
creation; it must not even seem to *be* creation. But the pseudofactual
mode, as intention, strategy, and effect, shuts off far more than just
the reader's delighted apprehension that he partakes of patterned,
purposeful fantasy. We shall see that Defoe's starting place prevents
him, for a long time, from expressing in fictional form his vision of
human experience. Profound meaning trails behind story, even until
Roxana.

Directions of Change

The second question is Defoe's destination. Obviously, having begun
writing what Ralph Rader calls "simulated naive incoherent autobiography," one appropriate direction for Defoe to go would be the

perfection of such a form: a book that despite its fictionality reads as if it is true, one that can covertly overcome, with its illusion, even a reader's extrinsic knowledge that the book is a fabrication. Such a work is *A Journal of the Plague Year*. To achieve it, Defoe turns back to what his predecessors had used so successfully, an actual event. He manages to induce the reader to accept the book as if it were a true account, to accept its referentiality, even though it is apparent Defoe wrote it.[29] The potentiality for such an effect was already available in *Robinson Crusoe*, but Defoe took some time to develop it. The *Journal*, I shall suggest, is the first in a long line of "fictions," such as *In Cold Blood* and *The Executioner's Song*, that depend on history.

At the same time, but with a reluctance born of his preference for history, Defoe moves toward incorporating positive evidence of fictionality into stories he continues to claim, in prefaces and on title pages, are true. Here there are a number of anomalies in one's intuitive experience of narrative, some of which Rader has pointed out only very recently.[30] Clearly, one recognizes as prose fictions some narratives one would feel uneasy calling novels: *Rasselas, Pilgrim's Progress, The Adventures of Master F. J., The Unfortunate Traveller*, and some more recent works like *Animal Farm*. More recently there is the "nonfiction novel." Apparently "prose fiction" is not at all synonymous with "novel." On the other hand, a body of works, dating from Richardson's *Pamela*, all share in common certain similarities that set them apart both from *Rasselas* and from most of Defoe's narratives. This other group might be called the traditional novel, so long as it is not assumed that the phrase is necessarily honorific. This form has been specified by Sheldon Sacks, who calls it the "represented action": "characters about whose fates we are made to care are introduced in unstable relationships which are then further complicated until the complications are finally resolved by the complete removal of the represented instability."[31] Put another way, traditional novels exhibit, along with much classical drama, a kind of teleological "tightness" that narrative before Richardson ordinarily does not; they are all closed, internally referring, probabilistic, causally patterned narratives we accept as avowed fictions. The inapplicability of the paradigm to most of Defoe, except *Roxana*, will be a continuing theme of this study.

But in the meantime, two other problems have arisen. One knows most of Defoe's narratives are fictions, or assumes them to be, but does one experience them as traditional novels? Certainly few readers hesitate to *call* them novels. Second, many works called novels do not yield easily to analysis as traditional novels, yet are clearly fictions. For one example, take the requirement that in the traditional novel episodes be motivated causally, that is, that the novel's plot reveal what at the level of the sentence we would call subordination. Novels as disparate as *Pamela, Tom Jones, Pride and Prejudice, Jude the Obscure*, and *One Flew Over the Cuckoo's Nest* all share this feature. Yet many other works referred to as novels have what one might call an additive structure, that "open form in which new peripeties can always be added to the end," as Victor Shklovsky noted, and which, as Todorov adds, corresponds to syntactic coordination.[32] Even these are not the only possibilities: for example, narrative can proceed by means of repetitive cycles, as *Tristram Shandy* does. There is no necessity, therefore, that what is called a novel reveal causal plotting. It may very well be that the traditional novel, which for Sacks was equivalent to *the* novel, is not the only type after all, and that some of Defoe's works, though not novels in the same sense that *Pamela* is, nevertheless satisfy some set of criteria that allow us to experience them as positively and not just accidentally fictional.

That these are not the only possible definitions of the novel I am well aware. But the combination of formal and psychological criteria brings us closer to what is going on in Defoe than definitions, like "realism," which, while less cumbersome, cannot provide the complex and continuing touchstone necessary to determine Defoe's ongoing development. It is not at all a denigration of Defoe's role in the rise of the traditional novel to say that he never wrote a coherent example of the form. The struggle he has to subdue his old intuitions of storytelling in order even to approach novelistic possibilities in

Roxana indicates what a giant step it was for narrative finally to adopt the probabilistic structures previously realized only in the drama and epic. Defining the novel, at least in its primary eighteenth- and nineteenth-century manifestations, as controlled and patterned representation that makes a virtue of obvious fictionality may exclude most of our favorite Defoe narratives; but we gain by that loss an understanding of the genesis of new forms.

The full account of Defoe's progressions must await succeeding chapters. But some general outline of his development, more adequate than what I have briefly suggested, is necessary before I turn to *Robinson Crusoe*. I have argued that one cannot understand Defoe apart from the dynamic relationship of his intentions, his forms, and the effects they imply. Yet even in specific passages, if their superficial homogeneity is penetrated, one can see Defoe doing different things in different places. With the risk of resembling Johnson's "pedant in *Hierocles*, who, when he offered his house to sale, carried a brick in his pocket as a specimen," I offer three examples. The first is from *A Journal of the Plague Year*.

> I might spend a great deal of Time in my Exclamations against the Follies, and indeed Wickedness of those things, in a Time of such Danger, in a matter of such Consequences as this, of a National Infection, But my Memorandums of these things relate rather to take notice only of the Fact, and mention that it was so: How the poor People found the Insufficiency of those things, and how many of them were afterwards carried away in the Dead-Carts, and thrown into the common Graves of every Parish, with these hellish Charms and Trumpery hanging about their Necks, remains to be spoken of as we go along.[33]

The narrator, whose impersonality is indicated by the fact that only his initials, H.F., are revealed at the very end of the *Journal*, is concerned here with the inefficacy of charms against the plague. He could rail against the foolishness of trusting to such superstition at a time when the sins of all were being judged. Instead, he lets the historical fact tell its own tale: those who trusted to anything but prayer, and even many of those, found themselves swept away by the pestilence. Defoe's interest, and the reader's, is not in a narrator's personal experience of death and horror, but in the manifestation itself: "the Fact," the "how" of the 1665 plague in London. The narrator serves as a particularly effective camera eye; he does not frequently inject his own judgments, even though he sorts out all kinds of conflicting opinions about the plague. His role is finally to enforce what every other element of the *Journal* also indicates: this is a real man recounting an historical event that he witnessed.

The second passage is from *Moll Flanders*, written the same year.

> I Sunk down when they brought me News of it, and after I came to myself again, I thought I should have died with the weight of it: My Governess acted a true Mother to me, she pittied me, she cryed with me, and for me; but she cou'd not help me; and to add to the Terror of it, 'twas the Discourse all over the House, that I should die for it; I cou'd hear them talk it among themselves very often; and see them shake their Heads, and say they were sorry for it, and the like, as is usual in the Place; but still no Body came to tell me their Thoughts, till at last one of the Keepers came to me privately, and said with a Sigh, well Mrs. *Flanders*, you will be tried a *Friday*, (this was but a *Wednesday*,) what do you intend to do? I turn'd as white as a Clout, and said, God knows what I shall do, for my part I know not what to do; why, *says he*, I won't flatter you, I would have you prepare for Death. [p. 282]

This, of course, is the sad culmination of Moll's career as a thief. The first thing to note about this passage is that it is a *scene*, with a personal dramatic quality H.F.'s narration lacks. Yet it is drama of a peculiar sort, the kind that only the fertile properties of narrative make possible: it is internal. It is as if the world—and Moll's is a cruel and unforgiving one—exists only to elicit her fascinating and quirky responses. It has objective existence, of course; but Moll is somehow a stranger to what goes on around her. She stands apart and watches as others discuss her probable fate. No one can help her, except to offer the dubious comfort of counseling preparation for the gibbet. She elsewhere calls herself an "indifferent Monitor," yet the title is inaccurate in many ways. She is probably as intensely responsive to her surroundings as any being in fiction. Even at points in her story where she seems merely an observer, she always relates the outside world to her precarious hopes and fears. Yet her receptivity creates only an illusion of interaction with the world and other people, the relationship by which character in the traditional novel is established, defined, and transmuted. Moll is simply, but delightfully, a carefully developed personage, a created psyche placed in as many different situations of stress as Defoe can invent. She fluctuates but does not change in any consistently recognizable way. Much more could be said about Moll. But for now, it is enough to recognize that she is a kind of epitome of the ways personality can be represented in real memoirs. One's sense of her, by design, remains floating, unpinned to any ulterior principle of progression, yet she is recognized as a fiction.

So far, then, there are Defoe's two primary strategies. The first is designed to ensure an unchallengeable illusion of literal verisimilitude. The second is a refinement of the attractions available in the literature of personality: diaries, memoirs, autobiographies. Both of these possibilities exist in *Robinson Crusoe*, as well as a third, one I shall call novelistic. This example is from *Roxana*.

> *Amy* was so provok'd, that she told me, *in short*, she began to think it wou'd be absolutely necessary to murther her: That Expression fill'd me with Horror; all my Blood ran chill in my Veins, and a Fit of trembling seiz'd me, that I cou'd not speak a good-while; at last, What is the Devil in you, *Amy, said I?* Nay, nay, *says she,* let it be the Devil, or not the Devil, if I thought she knew one tittle of your History, I wou'd dispatch her if she were my own Daughter a

thousand times; and I, *says I in a Rage*, as well as I love you, wou'd be the first that shou'd put the Halter about your Neck, and see you hang'd, with more Satisfaction than ever I saw you in my Life; nay, *says I*, you wou'd not live to be hang'd, *I believe*, I shou'd cut your Throat with my own Hand; I am almost ready to do it, *said I*, as 'tis, for your but naming the thing; with that, I call'd her cursed Devil, and bade her get out of the Room.

I think it was the first time that ever I was angry with *Amy* in all my Life; and when all was done, tho' she was a devilish Jade in having such a Thought, yet it was all of it the Effect of her Excess of Affection and Fidelity to me.

But this thing gave me a terrible Shock, for it happen'd just after I was marry'd, and serv'd to hasten my going over to *Holland*; for I wou'd not have been seen, so as to be known by the Name of *Roxana*, no, not for ten Thousand Pounds; it wou'd have been enough to have ruin'd me to all Intents and Purposes with my Husband, and everybody else too; I might as well have been the *German Princess*.[34]

The difference between this passage and the one from *Moll Flanders* is not primarily one of subject matter. In both, a threat looms that causes intense anxiety. There is, of course, much *more* going on here, the threat is more complex. Roxana is afraid that a daughter she long ago abandoned, and who has now unluckily turned up again, will reveal Roxana's tawdry past to her new husband, a man of admirable goodness and, above all, respectability. At the same time, Roxana fears what her friend-maid, Amy, might do to forestall the threat, which Amy perceives as a danger to her own position.

At this point, I have difficulties, because I cannot give a sense of the uniqueness of the situation without providing a detailed context for it. Yet the moment overall context, and not just the local episode, becomes important, one approaches novelistic effects. Roxana becomes an actress in a progressive, powerful sequence that will ultimately lead to her daughter's murder and Roxana's moral doom. There were *moments* of such narrative coalescence in earlier Defoe narratives. But only at the conclusion of *Roxana* do past and pre-sent—all that has happened to Roxana and all that she has become—interact to create a probable fate the quality of which we can experi-ence in advance. Narrative adventitiousness, suggestive of a chaotic world or at least of the chaotic nature of experience, has given way to pattern and order. The ordinary "and then, and then" of a Defoe narrative has yielded to a radically different teleology. Artlessness has become art or, as Murray Krieger put it, the "empirical world's *casual*" has become the novel's "causal."[35] Nature can no longer be exhibited by reference to mere "bricks."

These brief examples, and my comments, do not begin to suggest the complex transformations Defoe worked on the givens of his art. From fact to fiction, from the illusion of truth to structured fantasy, from ambiguity to determinate significance—these are some of the directions implied. When one turns to *Robinson Crusoe* and sees these impulses mingled, interpenetrating, frequently conflicting, and obeying no dictatorial injunction of the author, one begins to see why Defoe's development has continued hidden. In following his winding way we shall see an author working, often with only the faintest glimmer of any controlling intuition of form, toward ways of telling stories even he does not dream possible.

Throughout this study, there will appear to be some confusion over the term *novel*. I consistently suggest that Defoe's uses of narrative are usually not novelistic. Most of the time, what I intend to separate Defoe from is the body of works I have called the traditional novel. Yet, in another sense, there is a vital question underlying the problem over terminology. Might the concept of the novel be ulti-mately empty? If Rader can describe *Moll Flanders* as a "simulated . . . autobiography," and claim for it a kind of referential illusion, and still call it a novel, how useful is the concept? The problem cannot be solved here. Until the final chapter, where the explanatory adequacy of the categories of narrative will be taken up again, I shall use "novel" in the more restricted sense of meaning traditional novel, those works of prose fiction revealing strongly plotted, progressive structures, a group that is at least the most prominent subset of whatever the novel is.

II

"Robinson Crusoe"

EMPLOYING A METAPHOR, as was his wont, to describe narrative unity, Henry James likens *The Tragic Muse* to "some aromatic bag of gathered herbs of which the string has never been loosed."[1] The question of the final fragrance of the bouquet garni known as *Robinson Crusoe* continues to puzzle at least those students of narrative for whom deconstruction has not invalidated the whole enterprise. Clearly, any theory of narrative development concerned with wholes rather than parts, or even with the possibility of making wholes from parts, must consider the question, as well as the additional complication suggested by James's insistence on employing analogy: Is the unity so many have seen in Defoe's first major narrative a critical *ignis fatuus*, the delusive product of our continuing struggle to reduce chaotic stories to ordered patterns? Or is the book with all its admitted but remarkable "Variety," literally unified, every part, like Aesop's belly, "in its dull quiet way . . . doing necessary work for the body"?

The question of coherence floats around other issues that at first perusal do not seem to have much to do with it. For example, what else is at stake in the continuing disagreement about the very subject matter of *Robinson Crusoe*? Is it a story about solitary adventure, or religion, or economics, to take only the three top contenders? Does one really get anywhere if one must conclude, as did the most recent critic of the book, that it really is about both religion and economics, indeed that it is two stories? Certainly, two stories could coexist uneasily or somehow become a whole. But how? Allowing the two parts to live together, as this critic did, simply does not explain the wedding: unity is a question of the conditions of oneness, by definition.[2]

Not a few critics have been content to trace unity to Defoe's ideas. Aside from the almost universally held view of literature as a kind of special discourse, a view by no means originating with recent critics of narrative like Todorov,[3] there is some warrant for semantic abstraction in Defoe's stated practice. He consistently promulgated, in his prefaces and elsewhere, the neoclassical ideal of uniting "Diversion" and "Instruction" to generate a kind of sweet didacticism. It has therefore been the stated task of many Defoe critics to "show in detail how Defoe unites narration and instruction," a process that entails splitting asunder what Defoe joined. Occasionally a dissenting voice is heard. McKillop argues that "much of the time, of course, we see Crusoe merely following his 'rambling designs.' He does not always live in the presence of Fate or Providence." This is a sane view, but one that creates as many problems as it solves. For one, McKillop's thesis implies a lack of unity, ideological or otherwise, and in the sixties, at least in American criticism, organic criticism was all the rage, no matter how the coherence had to be located, or created. Most of the readings of Defoe's narratives arguing for some kind of semantic coherence come from that decade and are at least in part a reaction to McKillop. The second problem is related to, and actually the cause of, the first: thematic readings, generated as they are by analogically relating literal action to ideology, are *always* successful, at least on their own terms. McKillop's view, then, did not rule out further extraction of meaning but virtually guaranteed that it would take place. So it is that Watt, writing about the same time as McKillop, finds that the economic and not the spiritual dominates. The truths communicated beneath the smooth surface of narrative may differ from critic to critic, but the assumptions about narrative meaning remain fairly constant.[4]

That schemes as diverse as Providence, economic necessity, and "the idea of man's isolation" have arisen to explain the book does not necessarily require one to see *Robinson Crusoe* as fragmented, although that possibility always remains. The procession of competing readings, each somehow claiming authority over the whole, may be enough to cast doubt on Frank Ellis's sanguine statement that reading "the criticism of *Robinson Crusoe* since 1900 is almost enough to restore one's faith in progress."[5] Yet the causes of this plurality of meanings are not self-evident. Is it in the nature of texts, all texts, to mean diversely? Or is it in readers themselves? R. S. Crane, adapting Aristotle's methodological "pluralism," argued that no work of literature yields the same meaning when examined within different frameworks, a theory that seems to locate the problem not in the text but in the tools critics employ to understand it. Any critic can, therefore, select one aspect of *Robinson Crusoe* to subsume others, allusivity reaching, potentially, into all corners of the cosmos—a situation Tristram/Sterne would delight in, but one more than a little disturbing to a critic searching for probable knowledge about texts. This welter of competing readings, taken without logical warrant as evidence of textual treachery, then leads many critics to eschew the search for any sort of common ground in interpretation. In Frank Kermode's recent use of the terms, one must abandon plodding, "carnal" interpretation questing after shared literary experience and seek instead "spiritual" originality, the insight and even elegance of the personal vision.[6] The common assumption, one that is crucial to understanding how recent critics have approached Defoe, of both the unifiers and the deconstructionists, has been that narrativity is but one thing. One can even write a "poetics of prose," as if it really were a single thing (certainly a necessary precondition for Aristotle).[7] The novel, then, exhibits cohesion, or flies apart at the slightest touch, depending on one's prior constitution of what narrative is. Having made a prior commitment either to the order or, more commonly today, to the fragmentation of the world mirrored in narrative, one is prevented from even entertaining another possibility—that some narratives hold together and some do not. For better or worse, ontology once adopted limits the kinds of questions one can even entertain as significant.

Crane, whose work deserves more attention, actually set up three categories. Some works are unified but relatively barren, either of pleasure or significance (a number of eighteenth-century English tragedies come to mind). Others, also unified, are rich in local texture, abundantly satisfying Coleridge's standard of "the production of as much immediate pleasure in parts as is compatible with the largest sum of pleasure in the whole." Finally, still others "are rich in local virtues but have only a loose or tenuous overall form."[8] It is hardly surprising, since the New Critics in all their guises so assiduously studied their Coleridge, that the second category frequently seemed the only one worth bothering with and that, consequently, they frequently also found unity of some conceptual kind where more literal critics like Crane did not—as for example in the attempts to discover internal coherence in the *Canterbury Tales* or *In Our Time*. The quest for oneness as sole or even primary poetic virtue can mislead, especially if the goal is matter-of-fact, like understanding the development of discrete forms. One may learn more about the generation of new subspecies, within narrative as a whole, if one assumes that early examples have not always sprung forth fully mature and coherent. Early narrative comic development, for example, may be clearer after noting that Goldsmith did not entirely succeed in binding together the two halves of *The Vicar of Wakefield*. One then begins to understand how difficult it must have been in the middle eighteenth century in England to write a first-person comic action, in which moral ambiguities must be clarified by a narrator himself flawed in many ways. Goldsmith's shift to a more direct representation of moral values in the second half makes sense as the uneasy compromise with innovation one might expect from a friend of the man who wrote *Rasselas*.[9] In like manner, if one can accept as a possibility that *Robinson Crusoe* is pleasing because Defoe created a narrator who functions in several ways, one may begin to see how Crusoe can elicit so many responses, how each of his roles exerts its power on one's memory.[10] At times Crusoe is relatively unpersonalized, an "eye," or reporter; at others, he is a developed personage but not a novelistic character; and finally, at times Crusoe seems to interact in novellike sequences with other elements: thought and action. As obvious and unexciting as these functions may be, they hold the key to the mixed form of *Robinson Crusoe*—if "form" is not completely inappropriate, given the context. These roles neither provide a unifying scheme—one must, in fact, resist providing one by analogy in order to see their real importance—nor are they encompassed by something larger. They are not substructures, except in the barest and most critically fruitless sense of taking up space in the same book. Each use of Crusoe provides an isolable kind of narrative experience and a distinct kind of meaning. Each has been pulled out of the fluctuating context and employed as an organizing scheme.

More important for my thesis, the three uses parallel the three lines of development Defoe's narrative career followed. Narrative strategies originate as ways of dealing with remembered or created experience, ways that can vary drastically as the mind works on subject matter and considers effects. As strategies, the reportorial, the personal, and the interactive—to give them arbitrary names— therefore not only entail a number of varying formal relationships within the text, but also betoken significant differences in authorial attitude toward the text and in possibilities for the text as experience or use. For example, the Crusoe who is little more than an observer belongs to a very old tradition of *using* narrators; one does not ordinarily create a fictional narrator and then deprive him of significant traits of personality unless he is to serve a function conceived of as more important than the representation of personality. This Crusoe leads, by clear steps, to the determinate, referential significance of the *Memoirs of a Cavalier* and *A Journal of the Plague Year*. The Crusoe who is a product of Defoe's "keen eye for traits of character and a very vivid idea of persons"[11] becomes Moll, Colonel Jack, and the Roxana of most of her story, refinements of personality and epitomes of the pleasures possible in earlier works, such as real memoirs, that concentrated on the inner lives of diarists or autobiographers. Here is, not novelistic character, but "consciousness," following the sense of John Bayley's distinction. Finally, during brief sequences—Defoe never wrote a coherent traditional novel—Crusoe participates in what Bayley calls "a complex process of rapport between author and ourselves" by which "we know what to think" of him and his story.[12] This last usage of Crusoe is not easy to locate, in part because Defoe does all he can to hide it, destructive as it is of the illusion of factuality. In brief sections, however, Defoe experiments with the kind of control that will culminate in the novelistic conclusion of *Roxana*, not to mention other protonovelistic sequences scattered throughout the other books. Once these separate impulses are discriminated and their importance for the novel articulated, McKillop's contention that Defoe did not advance by "artistic self-discovery" becomes untenable, but for the most literal understanding of "discovery" as being always intellectual and conscious.

Had Defoe written the *Memoirs of a Cavalier* or *A Journal of the Plague Year* before *Robinson Crusoe*, at least one line of his development would long ago have been recognized. Those two later works clearly make virtues of what in the earlier work are minor annoyances, Crusoe's "rambling." The *Memoirs* and the *Journal* are coherent and successful imitations of true stories, and therefore rest securely in a tradition much older than Defoe. With its alternating intentions intertwined and blended into effects suspended often between potentiality and realization, Crusoe's story seems to mock efforts to specify its teleology. Nor is the problem merely one of subject, the variety Defoe seems to have had in mind as he went about collecting or inventing Crusoe's early "strange surprizing adventures." The process of "communication," as Wolfgang Iser terms it, is also confused.[13] Apart from the few times Crusoe acts in a context that

30

allows the reader to infer specific information—for example, the sequence of fear-longing-action involving the cannibals—one's responses are usually "free" to a large extent. In his reportorial and personal uses, Crusoe remains a potential vehicle for whatever idiosyncratic interpretation individual associations produce. Some degree of significant common response to Crusoe is possible only when Defoe novelistically "pins" Crusoe's developing hopes and fears causally to a situation qualitatively predictable. Crusoe yearns, after years on the island, for the sound of just one voice other than his own; but when visitors finally come, they are the ghastliest of human outcasts, cannibals. He is torn between two powerful impulses of attraction and repulsion, with his desire for contact winning out—it will later be seen how—only after a long period. Just how important this careful "justification" of Crusoe's actions, necessarily involving the taking of life, was to the overall aims of the episode can be seen by the effect it had on many viewers of a public-television version of the book a few years ago. What had required a careful juxtaposition of narrative reasons in order not to seem gratuitous violence now became exactly that: Crusoe attacks because his little kingdom has been threatened by the black savages, and his slaughter of them seemed to be a vicious manifestation of imperialist racism. Crusoe, if not Defoe, may *be* a racist, but the point is that in the midst of this sequence such a judgment has been precluded. Most of the time, however, when Crusoe is just an observer or is vividly but not causally involved in the action sequence, it is impossible to speak of any reader's "appropriate" much less "necessary" reaction to him. And if the text asserts no tyranny, benevolent or otherwise, as the traditional novel does, with all its loose ends, how can the reader determine its meaning? The text itself turns treacherous, as some recent criticism would have it for all narrative.

The problem with Crusoe, however, is not that his story partakes of some special liability to indeterminacy peculiar to narrative in general, but that sometimes Defoe controls with a certain degree of success all the eclectic diversity of the sequence and sometimes he simply refuses to subordinate his materials to a probabilistic pattern. The "Editor" of Crusoe's words tells the reader that this is the "Story" of a "private Man's Adventures," involving "Wonders" that are "scarce capable of greater Variety." Yet "story" is not quite right, since there is no "Appearance of Fiction" in it; it is rather a "just History of Fact,"[14] an emphatic formulation in light of how much weight "just" carried with all neoclassical critics, including Johnson. Clearly, one is faced here with two orders of probability. The first and least common in *Robinson Crusoe* demands that the reader experience Crusoe, at least tacitly, as an artificial construct in a fabricated structure. This view receives confirmation as well as an indeterminate measure of complication from the external knowledge that the whole *is* in fact a fabrication. The second order, introduced and bolstered by title page and preface, requires unambiguously that Crusoe be regarded as a natural person. The distinction is obvious, although it is usually ignored as unimportant, especially since the reader knows the book is a fiction. Yet books do not usually require readers, in effect, to alternate between knowing fully the psyche of a character in order that they may participate in the progression of which he is a subordinated element and, at other times, allowing him the natural opacity, the secrecy, of real people. Indeed, few readers can read the book this way, requiring as it does almost a somatic contradiction, and fewer probably would want to if they could.

The result has been that, appetites honed by expectation of full fictional revelation of character, and the "true story" actually hiding more than it reveals, readers have been forced to construe for themselves, to manufacture, a consistent inner life and ethical being for a Crusoe who does not literally reveal such consistency. This makes *Robinson Crusoe* sound very "modern" in its indeterminacy and capacity for duplicity. The problem is that, with the model of novelistic development I have sketched, this is the opposite direction Defoe should have taken had he wanted to reach the much more determinate significance of the traditional novel. While the formulation may seem both solipsistic and egregiously self-confirming, it is based on literary history. One may, of course, interpret even strong systems such as *Pamela* and *Tom Jones* as freely as one chooses. But to the extent that they are systems, the traditional novel after Richardson was not in the business of mystification but revelation. When readers are confused, about Lovelace or Stephen Dedalus, disclosure is inadequate. Indeed, one definition of the action novel, and one indication of how much its birth owes to the importation of semiological strategies from the drama, would be that it is a system strong enough to mold shared belief, if only for the story's time being. Other works that are recognized as fictions exert no such power, or do so feebly. True stories, or imitated ones, do not do so either, but not by choice: natural people hold close to their motivations and their private chronicles often hide more than they reveal. Still other works, like *Robinson Crusoe*, embody an impossible formal "request," that the reader experience them as both true and fabricated.

This phenomenological problem has its moral side, since Defoe goes on in his preface to suggest that, while this is a true story, with a principle of "Diversion," yet overall rules a didactic intention, "a religious Application of Events to the Uses which wise Men always apply them." Then follows another bifurcation, since the moral consists of Crusoe's negative example, his disobedience, as well as his fate, his final deliverance, intended "to justify and honour the Wisdom of Providence" (p. 1). Just as readers' merest instrumental judgments of Crusoe lack moorings at times, their involvement in his moral plight fails of direction and coherence as well when Defoe places his character on the page virtually deprived of a signifying context. Didacticism, certainly of Defoe's plain sort, cannot emerge from such a silence, and events decidedly do not speak for themselves. Yet it would be inaccurate to conclude from this formal and moral liability that Defoe himself has lost touch with the ethical implications of Crusoe's plight. Not only do stories have expectations for readers, they have them for their creators as well, as Sartre reminded us in *What Is Literature?* If the intention to replicate a true story does not require a coherent configuration of subordinated belief, if, in fact, such belief could destroy the illusion, can an author be blamed for not behaving novelistically? The answer is, of course, that he *can*, but should not, be blamed, if only because it is more interesting to see what sorts of semantic blind alleys Defoe leads his reader into than it is to impose some analogical scheme that makes "sense" of the confusion. Crusoe, for example, swears one moment that his companion in escape from slavery, Xury, showed him "so much Affection" that Crusoe had to "love him ever after" (p. 25); ten pages later Crusoe has sold him for sixty pieces of eight, with the eleemosynary stipulation that the boy will gain his freedom in ten years if he turns Christian. The juxtaposition seems inadvertent, even unsavory— until one realizes that it literally has no *purpose*. This is not the same as saying it is inadvertent, which would imply a standard of proceeding that would make of such a contradiction an excrescense. When Defoe's mind is on using Crusoe, or any of his narrators, as reporter— as witness of "wonders"—he thinks only of traits of personality as plausible means of transition. He is not "distanced" from Crusoe, as Joyce is from Stephen; he simply does not think of him as a consistent character. How different such a moment is from the cannibal sequence, in its demands on both Defoe and the reader, should be obvious if somewhat unsettling. Defoe's imagination is no more with Crusoe the "reporter" than it was to be with the Cavalier.

The reportorial strategy even requires that the personality Defoe might routinely endow with vividness be muted in order to maintain the illusion of truth. Regardless, whether Crusoe's aimlessness results from Defoe's adherence to an older tradition, from a fixation on the integrity of "the event," or from a desire to replicate quotidian randomness, in the absence of a pervasive and recognizable teleology, Defoe's values remain unknowable unless they are sought outside the fiction—a practice entailing its own hazards. The novel-to-come would utilize value in a radically different way, subordinating it to a strong sequence of action and character having determinate significance. Such, at least, is the novel's intention, even if no novel perfectly achieves it. Having rejected satire—Defoe was not very good at it, although he handled other kinds of irony and invective skillfully[15]—as well as more direct narrative means for conveying beliefs, such as Bunyanesque allegory and the sort of parable or apologue form Johnson used so effectively, Defoe leaves himself little direction to go except toward the novel. Replicating the forms and effects of true stories means relinquishing the possibilities for conveying a moral vision, although one can always simply "insert" beliefs, if care is taken not to appear too systematic. When one merely endows a narrator with a personality, frequently pays it only fitful attention, and avoids the creation of significant interaction with the "and then, and then" of the story, the Horatian ideal falters in practice. Drama, with its commitment to public fictionality and formal structure, proffers its patterned fable unabashedly. But Defoe distrusted drama, although he seems to have liked it well enough.[16] His clinging to the pseudofactual mode seems indeed to be a kind of reaction against the "untruths" of drama so many critics had railed at during Defoe's lifetime. Yet his doing so is ironic in that his seeking a more moral, because truer, genre leads not only to duplicity but to moral ambiguity. True stories often leave meaning to the reader. Interpretation of fictional narrative may be difficult, especially in regard to values. But what standard of meaning resides in narrative propositions that purport merely to be true? "Lee Harvey Oswald killed John F. Kennedy"—a narrative statement, calling not for interpretation but simple verification. Once the "fact" was established, a context for the determination of meaning might be available. But *Robinson Crusoe* begs even this question, since Defoe was careful to distance the story from the real events it vaguely resembles—the Selkirk story.

The novel creates and insists on its own artificial context, which is why, perhaps, in all its variations it seems to some unsuited to modern value chaos. Defoe's approximation to novelistic effects can be tested by comparing most of his works to McKillop's formulation of his practice.

> The simplest or minimum form of impersonation consists in providing a reporter or narrator who may appropriately give the details in

his own way. This is a natural mode of journalism, and admits of considerable variety of intention. . . . We then proceed in the great fictions to the stage at which the impersonated reporter tells how he was forced to deal with pressing circumstances affecting his own survival or success; the interplay between the impersonated character and the circumstance gets us into a kind of circle, with each giving significance to the other.[17]

It is impossible to dispute at least the partial accuracy of this description of Defoe's practice, although McKillop leaves out a number of steps in the process and it is hard to predict exactly how Defoe's own beliefs would function in the "interplay." But despite my agreement with McKillop, I cannot see much resemblance between the most complex "interplay" and what ordinarily goes on in the novel. Much the commonest case in Defoe, in addition, is for the "circle" to remain firmly closed and resistant to interpretation. A created personage can interact with his or her environment for hundreds of pages through dozens of fascinating episodes, pronouncing all sorts of verdicts on questions of every kind, and one still does not have the novel. The traditional novel attempts to subordinate the interaction among character, event, and belief to something else, a pattern of represented experience that allows the reader continuing knowledge of the qualitative nature of the pattern itself: a novel of this traditional sort includes beliefs, as it includes everything else, to achieve a predictable and satisfying resolution of instability. Such "neatness" may now be distasteful, but the action novel displayed it. Pamela, for example, finally marries her Squire B. and all her troubles seem over. Except the reader knows they are not, and so did Richardson. The novel must go on, because all the issues are not resolved. The issues, of course, are not ideological but experiential. While readers recognize that marriage to the Squire is best for Pamela, given the odious alternatives, they also know that "best" does not mean "ideal" in Richardson's moral world. I can use such terms of cognitive certainty as "know" and "recognized" because the novel in Richardson's hands presents branching alternatives to the characters, each choice charged with ethical implication because of the traits Richardson has called to the forefront in each character. One knows, therefore, not necessarily *what* the outcome of pattern will be, even before the marriage, but that whatever it is, it will involve a shade of moral gray, the ethical ambiguity Sheldon Sacks notes is characteristic of the action-type he calls "serious," as opposed to the comic and tragic.[18] Yet the ambiguity residing in the conclusion of *Pamela* results precisely because we have such a quantity of specifiable knowledge about the deficiencies and strengths of character Squire B. and even dear Pamela have shown us. In the serious action, then, ambiguity can result as a positive consequence of the form. While Pamela's character seemed ambiguous to Fielding, in quite different terms, *that* ambiguity was not a positive, intended consequence of the novel's form.

Such is not the case with most parts of *Robinson Crusoe*. Too often the reader's simplest judgments of better or worse are confused or blocked for lack of evidence and one must, to create the meaning that is not found, yoke traits of personality to events that finally are not mutually illuminating. Causality is a chimera and will remain so until Defoe discovers a narrative structure that makes a positive virtue of represented beliefs.

It might be argued that in my single-minded pursuit of what Defoe does *not* do, I have forgotten that an author's refusals and renunciations are themselves positive evidence of an important sort. We shall see later on that this is the case, that Defoe's consistent refusal to utilize belief positively does imply much about his view of art and the world. But that is not the question now. Only a knowledge of what the novel was to be can allow critics to dispense with the erroneous view of Defoe as one who refused to judge his material— rather than, as I am arguing, an author who refuses to write works that require precise judgment. Nevertheless, *Robinson Crusoe* does contain sequences that tease with their novelistic tendencies. Only by seeing how short they stop can one understand where Defoe's real interest and talent lie, in the creation of personality. The third strategy, the reportorial, actually takes up little space, although Defoe will later isolate and use it almost exclusively in such nonnovels as the *Journal* and the *Memoirs*. Each of the three has its counterpart in later fiction. A Pamela or Pip can "step back" from the flow of events and comment in more or less neutral ways, although the aims of the traditional novel imply the elimination of anything inert. Then, too, narrators can give an impression of being intensely human without their humanity affecting the progress of the fable, at least in any causal fashion. Probably every traditional novel contains at least one character who exists only so that the reader may take pleasure in the portrayal (although one would look long and hard for such an unsubordinated element in most of Jane Austen's novels). This lucid and mutable aura, floating free, characterizes many real memoirs and some twentieth-century lyric novels, such as Virginia Woolf's, that enlist autobiography in the service of fiction. Character implies reintegration; not only the representation of traits must take place, but those traits must lead somewhere qualitatively determined. To suggest that Defoe, much less Virginia Woolf, did not create character may seem absurdly perverse. The terms are not important; I wish only to point out significant differences occurring on both ends of the development of traditional novelistic types.

If one accepts this view of traditional character as an element in a progressive action, then Defoe created few examples of character. In the novel, the "I" reveals himself, or is revealed by a narrator, so that the reader may understand and even anticipate what the "I" is to become. The world of the novel indeed implies a connection between what one has been and what one will be in the future. Whether the movement is from happiness to misery, the reverse, or some other significant transmutation of status, character, or belief, the fate of a character in an action results as no matter of chance even, in what only masquerades as a paradox, if events fall out from "Fortune." Fielding manages to attain a kind of high and serious decorum with his ludicrous tale of Tom in part because the ordered comic world of *Tom*

Jones implies an external world of moral and social chaos.[19] The novel depends on a belief in order. Even Hemingway, whose universe was populated by no gods, benevolent or malign, abided in the clean well-lighted place of art. The novel, then, demands that the people of the book not simply reside as nonpaying guests but contribute their share to the upkeep of the story. It will only be Defoe's discovery of how to reintegrate into the flow of narrative previously revealed information about Roxana that will permit him to approach the threshold of the novel. In *Robinson Crusoe* the three uses of the narrator remain disjoined, as if Defoe contented himself, in this his first effort, with their exemplification. He has created a structure of sorts, but one that makes no systematic use of anything but the moral commonplaces of the age.

Reportage

A sense of "this really happened" does not arise solely from eliminating all traces of selfhood in a narrator. Aristotle noted that even a blatantly fictional genre like tragedy could do without character; many of the actual memoirs we most value, on the contrary, charm us with their idiosyncratic "narrators." Crusoe, however, seems frequently to view events only to describe them. Though not the only response to such narrative inertia, credence of a rather passive sort is the obvious one. Crusoe, for example, even describes his own past as if he is speaking about another (which, in one sense, he is). He was born "in the Year 1632, in the City of *York*," his father originally "of *Bremen*, who settled first at *Hull*." Crusoe relates that his father left off trade, moved to York, and married a woman named Robinson. The family name, originally Kreutznaer, became by "the usual Corruption of Words" Crusoe (p. 3). As wooden as this memorial reconstruction is, it does not stifle inferential activity by the reader. Instead, it encourages it, readers being forced to scurry about to find *any* meaning here, in Crusoe's foreign heritage, change of name, or even his calling his family "good." But a functional, "carnal" interpretation of this passage—which comes close to being noninterpretation—would remain content, if not excitedly eager, to stress that these details merely reinforce the insistence of the preface that the book is what it claims, a "just History of Fact."

A century ago, most critics believed that this pseudofactual strategy was Defoe's only one, a view repeated in much more sophisticated form recently by Rader.[20] The use of Crusoe as impersonal chronicler of unsystematized experience is actually as rare in his story as it is common in earlier narrative and in Defoe's own *Journal* and *Memoirs of a Cavalier*. Nevertheless, it is clear, as Wordsworth once observed to Reverend Graves, that Defoe creates what personality Crusoe has, at least initially, in order to "decorate" the book's main attraction: the exfoliation of the island scenes of isolation. Wordsworth even pinpoints what would later become a major strategy of the comic novel: "the high pleasure derived from his successes and good fortunes arose from the peculiar source of these uncommon merits of his character"—here is the basis of *Tom Jones*, the dynamic tension between merit and expected fate that informs the book's structure and is the basis of its effect.[21] Defoe does not, of course, provide such a relationship with a direction, but leaves it as a fascinating interplay. Fielding and Austen will exhibit "uncommon merits" and involve the character in a dynamic instability leading in a probable manner to resolution and reward. In Defoe, at least until *Roxana*, where the proposition is moral doom and not felicity, the connection between what a personage deserves and what he or she gets is tenuous indeed. Certainly, Crusoe becomes more vitally human, and therefore more interesting, when he washes up on the island and the clichés of reportorial adventure can be left behind. Even so, once he leaves the island, he reverts back to the personal cipher he was before, and the interplay McKillop notes as characteristic of Defoe fades away.

The shift is a bit puzzling; but then again, the decision to continue the book after the rescue, a promising natural device of closure, is itself perplexing. Crusoe settles his affairs in Lisbon and decides to set out for London by land. As usual when Defoe's people travel, the reason for this decision comes, not from any deep motive, but from an arbitrary inclination given only token attention. It is quirky, of course, that he says he had a "strange Aversion to going to *England* by Sea," but if one asks why he had gained such an aversion, the answer is so obvious some may want to create a more complex one. Here the dual nature of the book comes out clearly. Some readers will explain Crusoe's decision on the basis of his unpleasant past experiences at sea—that is, *within* the illusion of factuality; others will argue that Defoe had some land adventures on the Continent he wanted to use to pad the story—they view the book as created and not "remembered." Although Crusoe assures his readers he will not "trouble" them with his "Land-Journal," there are "some Adventures" he "must not omit" (pp. 288–289). So now the solitary speaker who forms the heart of Defoe's greatest stories recedes into the anonymity of the traveling party, the pronouns shift from "I" and "me" to "we" and "us", and events wrestle the story away from the narrator. For example, Friday decides to tease a large bear, to the surprise of no one more than the reader; after all, where has Friday ever even seen a bear before? From the sequence comes only the most minimal sense of discrete personality, and such apparently was Defoe's intention. Crusoe imparts the quality of the collective experience: "we had laughing enough . . . we thought he depended on shaking the Bear off . . . we found the Bear too cunning for that too . . . *Friday* put us out of doubt" (p. 296). The vibrancy of Crusoe's interactive personality has been stilled beneath the weight of "adventures" that do not even have novelty to justify their existence. Defoe could not have invented a better way to preclude any strong sense of completeness and closure. The flat stretching out of the book, and the sequent *Farther Adventures*, with its wearisome string of "wonders" during which Crusoe's role is little more than that of a somewhat insensitive tour guide, suffers from the insipidity of so much previous "travel lie." The scenes before and after the island are little better, although, Crusoe having once been seen busy in his paradise, any episode of which he is a part contains some interest. Even so, everything in the book except the island sequence is nonsense that should have been excised,[22] Rousseau thought. Of course, if Defoe had been writing a traditional novel, Rousseau would have been correct. The *Farther Adventures* provides the best evidence that Defoe did not conceive of Crusoe in pervasively spiritual terms, or in any other single-minded fashion. Nothing could be farther from Defoe's mind as he leads Crusoe around the world, in a clear attempt to capitalize on the success of part one, than Crusoe's relationship with his God.

One can only speculate as to why Defoe sometimes choked off the imaginative flow that gives life to his narrators. In part it is the fear of his audience crying "Romance" at the evidence of fabulation. It may be a fascination with geography. For whatever reasons, it is curious that Defoe's travelers are least vivid when they *are* traveling: Crusoe before and after the island, and in the second part; Singleton crossing Africa; Jack on his later trading cruises. Scenic these sections may be, but the impulse toward vivid portrayal of personality has somehow been superseded. One difference between Moll and Roxana and all of Defoe's other narrators is that Defoe's two female narrators, despite all their peregrinations, always remain the center of attention, to the extent that their consciousness provides virtually a principle of unity. Society and geography never succeed in displacing them, even when, as with Moll in America, one might expect Defoe's attention to be deflected from his narrator's personality. But Moll and Roxana are unusual; they seem to have gripped Defoe's attention more firmly than the others did. Defoe's development is in part a growing ability to reject these tempting episodes of "true adventure" in favor of representing the inner life, a movement away from "history" and the supremacy of events and toward psychology. This movement is not identical to the rise of the novel, but since the great strength of narrative would come to be the representation of internal states of being, it is a step toward the novel.

What the inert passages of *Robinson Crusoe* may have taught Defoe, with the help of Charles Gildon, was the necessity of building more intrinsic interest into the subject matter if he was going to limit his narrator's role to that of a recording device. This necessity leads to the *Journal*, by way of the Cavalier's *Memoirs*, so that the failure or inherent deficiency of the pseudofactual, reportorial mode was, in this regard, fortuitous.

Personality

One comes to know novelistic acquaintances much as one does real people, inferring probabilities or receiving explicit information. In life, perhaps, the signs are always ambiguous and what is told, more or less unreliable. The patterns and profundities of real people are manifestly untrustworthy. The most firmly held beliefs of a lifetime can be discarded overnight. In the traditional novel, both consistency and complexity are intended to be recognized and understood; characters, even if they are unreliable, are reliably so. One constitutes their being with confidence even by virtue of their deviousness. Between these poles of life and highly structured narrative exist many variant possibilities for freedom and indeterminancy on the one hand, and structure and coherent meaning on the other. As Defoe manipulates Crusoe to varying ends, including portraying him for the sheer documentary pleasure of the portrayal itself, Crusoe moves now toward the older factual forms, now toward the novel, in which personage takes on the bound status of character. Meaning varies on the same continuum, although not always in parallel ways.

Even when Crusoe's vision focuses on the intrinsic interest of the object or task in front of him, Defoe frequently specifies thought and emotion. Those traits, however, consistently elicit what James Sutherland has called "delight in experience for its own sake," a possibility more recent critics, with their biases in favor of ideological meaning, have not been willing to consider seriously. Defoe, never one to ignore the shortest way to his readers' hearts, supplied what had been missing from most earlier narratives of travel and adventure: the mimetic recreation—although it was to seem merely reported—of "the human delight in making things."[23] Crusoe says of his pot making, "It would make the Reader pity me, or rather laugh at me to tell how many awkward ways I took to raise this Paste, what odd mishapen ugly things I made, how many of them fell in, and how many fell out" (p. 120). The juxtaposition of whimsicality with the situation of need assures the reader simultaneously of the comic futility—"laugh"—and vital importance—"pity"—of constructing "two large earthern ugly things . . . in about two Months Labour" (p. 120). While we enjoy Crusoe's retrospective distance in itself—it is fascinating to watch someone judge an earlier version of himself—it serves here mainly to heighten interest in the activity. From such a fortuitous dovetailing of activity, rather than any mere accretion of details, issues the attraction of many of the island scenes of survival and resourcefulness. It is this "standard of appropriateness" Defoe momentarily forgets when he allows event to override personality.

Refining this matching of personality and event finally leads to Defoe's most common and most successful strategy, to the harmonious relationship between Moll and, paradoxically, a hostile society. She is, it is often said, exactly what someone would have to be to get along in that world. Such a use of personage also runs little risk of subverting the factual illusion, so long as relatively inert passages of reportage are intermingled. It is also a short and perhaps logical step from using personage to highlight events to unearthing situations in which personality can be shown off, captured in all its multifariousness. Defoe's celebration of variety in all the prefaces except the one to *Roxana* becomes then something more than a neoclassical cliché, since not only many experiences but a number of ways to experience narrative itself have been built in. It is in this sense that Defoe is most clearly an innovator: writers before him tended, like Bunyan, to narrate in only one mode. This is not to say that Defoe would not have found earlier examples of most of his strategies. The passive sense of personality Crusoe sometimes exhibits occurs frequently in French pseudomemoirs such as those of Courtilz.[24] Only a lack of knowledge about these earlier performances, many of which Defoe knew well, has allowed critics of the English narrative tradition even to consider the hypothesis that Defoe is doing something completely new. Some of these earlier works closely resemble the illusory historicity of Defoe's *Memoirs of a Cavalier*, at least to the extent that they subordinate personality to event.

A few, however, like Courtilz's *Memoires de le Comte de Rochefort*, translated in 1696, are much closer to Defoe's effects than most critics of Defoe have recognized, and probably influenced Defoe's own methods. In 1704 Defoe summarized a long episode from the book, clearly echoing the translation. It was a "history," one he believed true, which he had on his mind for decades, since he paraphrases the title two years after *Roxana* in *The Political History of the Devil* (1726). *Rochefort* purports to be, like so many of Courtilz's other "memoirs," the self-revelations of a public figure, in this case one who hovered just beneath the greatness of Mazarin and Richelieu. From the beginning, however, what fascinates Courtilz is not the external event but Rochefort's response to it, the emotions and thoughts that show him to be a man and not just a political chesspiece. Before Courtilz the choice of first-person narration was, except in the picaresque, primarily a device of illusion; someone telling his own story could be trusted. But Courtilz tries to find ways to make point of view an artistic virtue as well. Even when political intrigue concerns him most, he is careful to dramatize its effect on his narrator's consciousness. Ostensibly, the reason for this narrowed focus is Rochefort's resolve "to speak of nothing but what I had a hand in my self," a motto and point of view appropriate as well to Moll. Once this intention translates into a consistent principle of progression, nothing Rochefort relates, no matter how objectively digressive, will seem excrescent if Courtilz invents a corrolary psychological state.

If not new, the technique is at least unusual. Much early narrative precludes any apprehension of digression by virtue of its tenuous unity. Yet if one defines unity as some principle that makes a virtue of every element of action, character, thought, technique, and language—as Aristotle does for tragedy—*Rochefort* still does not exhibit unity. It has a loose standard of appropriateness, but no continuing standard of probability, much less necessity. Rochefort, for example, goes out into the streets during a riot, is recognized by the mob as one who "had suffer'd deeply by the Tyranny of *Mazarin*," and is solicited by the mob to be its captain. The narrator's eyes seem to be solely on the events: "This disturbance would have run further, if the Queen Mother, who had before refus'd to set at liberty those she had made Prisoners, had not now been better advis'd; but she releast them, and every one went home quickly." This has the anticlimactic ring of a real event, as many of Defoe's pseudofactual works like the *Memoirs* do. But Courtilz immediately goes on to tie events to their effect on his narrator: "I was afraid however, that this matter would be a new Cause of Quarrel at me; and in short I made no question, having been so rudely handled by Mazarin already, but he would accuse me now of having been a Ringleader in the public tumult. . . . I thought it my best way to get some Protection."[25] Events and response exhibit no novelistic symbiosis here, they have been related by pairing. In addition, since Rochefort did live and was a public figure, Courtilz is a bit limited in the thoughts he can ascribe to him, so that Rochefort's responses frequently have the quality of predictability one would expect from an author not free to imagine human idiosyncrasy, as Defoe is. The direction of subordination, however, is the same, events yielding their importance to the representation of the inner life.

In seventeenth-century narrative there are fewer examples than one might expect of this interlocking of psyche and situation. For an author to subordinate the public, social reality in which his creations move to the depiction of personality, he must believe that the solitary soul is somehow more important, or at least more interesting, when singled out from its surroundings. Yet even an intensely sociological genre like the picaresque, in which personality usually serves to expose the viciousness and depravity of individuals and institutions that would deny the narrator his daily bread, shows this same tendency to mutate toward exhibiting the individuality of a narrator created to satirize. *Lazarillo de Tormes*, for example, is an early instance of the uneasy truce between function—a narrator turned to ideological use—and mimesis—representation for its own sake—that exists in much early narrative and that provides therefore a paradigm for understanding Defoe. Beginning perhaps as a collection of separate "jokes," or *chistes*, centered around a folkloric hero, *Lazarillo* exfoliated as the author created a narrator whose vision would serve as a device of linkage. "Little Lazarus" even displays a certain amount of moral development through the first three parts, at which point the satiric intention, never completely absent, reasserts itself in the final sections. Lazarillo stands back and dispassionately relates the corruption of his world. Personality becomes reportage, involvement yields to objective and distanced observation—the exigencies of effective storytelling give way to strategies of exposure and attack directed at targets outside the represented world of the book.

Between *Lazarillo* (1554) and Defoe, many other narratives would contain the same tension between function and representation. Narrators might not always be designed originally for satiric use, but frequently they would take on independent life. Don Quixote himself commences his fictional life as little more than a convenient device for Cervantes to ridicule the more egregious sins of the romance tradition. By the end of his story he is much more. Cervantes has, while "using" him as a tool of satire, gained a respect for his independent integrity.[26] It may be that there is something inevitable about this liberation of narrative from the confines and demands of referentiality, either satiric or didactic, if only because the nature of the medium, combined with the first-person point of view developed originally for purposes of factual illusion, lends itself especially well to imitating the vagaries of personality. Courtilz is a kind of bridge, continuing to use his narrators to create an illusory historicity while searching within those constraints for enough freedom to endow them with prominent inner life. Even so, seldom does Courtilz stray very far from the pseudofactual conventions, ones only slightly less inflexible than those of epic and tragedy.[27]

Defoe reveals the same tensions. At the beginning of *Robinson*

Crusoe, despite the situation of stress between Crusoe and his father, what one sees are little more than the hackneyed clichés of so many previous voyage narratives. Crusoe's "rambling Thoughts" leave him "satisfied with nothing but going to Sea" (p. 3), despite his father's sane expostulations. Certainly nothing like an inward colloquy of Crusoe's doubts in response to his father's urgings ever develops, the entire sequence serving as economically as possible to get the narrator off to sea and away from the unpromising "Peace and Plenty" of his father's "middle Station of Life" (p. 5). The father's objections are listed en masse without reply from Crusoe until the rather predictable, "I was sincerely affected with this Discourse, as indeed who could be otherwise?" (p. 6). One recent critic has argued that *Robinson Crusoe* is the first novel precisely because Crusoe refuses to heed advice and remain at home, otherwise there would be no story.[28] But this is to talk about Crusoe as if he were a natural person, admittedly a strong temptation. Defoe can commence the story anywhere he pleases, so there must be a reason for starting with "disobedience," apart from the rather unimportant one that earlier adventure stories often began with the hero's childhood. Leo Braudy, reacting to the numerous "spiritual" readings of the book, has suggested that one can make too much of Crusoe's disobedience, that to style it "original sin" is taking "all authority to be equivalent." Defoe's antagonist, Charles Gildon, said much the same thing in his satire of *Robinson Crusoe*: "I dare believe that there are few Men who consider justly, that would think the Profession of a *Yorkshire* Attorney more innocent and beneficial to Mankind than that of a Seaman, or would judge that *Robinson Crusoe* was so very criminal in rejecting the former, and chusing the latter, as to provoke the Divine Providence to raise two Storms, and . . . destroy so many Ships and Men, purely to deter him from that Course of Life."[29]

Yet Crusoe's retrospective rhetoric of doom clearly indicates that *he* looks on his original actions as entailing the misery that befell him: "I would be satisfied with nothing but going to Sea . . . against the Will, nay the Commands of my Father . . . there seem'd to be something fatal in that Propension of Nature tending directly to the Life of Misery which was to befal me" (p. 3). Looking back on a life that included twenty-six years of solitude, it is appropriate that he see his first step toward that exile as somehow a serious mistake. Yet to generalize from this loose appropriateness the conclusion that Crusoe is some sort of driven, compulsive capitalist, as Watt does, seems an unwarranted abstracting and distancing of what serves, as an ideational element not fully synthesized, a number of much more specific purposes. In addition, whatever burden of years Crusoe spent on his island, it was undoubtedly too heavy a price to pay for anyone to argue seriously that he "actually gains by his 'original sin.' "[30] It is no denigration of Defoe's purpose, much less his achievement, to see this rhetoric of sin and repentance as serving something other than a serious and pervasive spiritual intention.

For one thing, as Rader has pointed out, Defoe knew that by including elements readers were familiar with from veritable spiritual autobiographies he could reinforce the illusion of truth. There are other reasons, some relatively minor, some fairly important— none, however, indicates that these ideological elements compose the radical basis of the book. Least important as a reason for his "obstinacy" is that it gives Defoe a plausible reason to get Crusoe on his way. Secondly, Crusoe's "serious reflections" on his past conduct throughout the book allow for an illusion of character progression within what is objectively a static sequence. Then, too, given the mundane nature of his island activities, Defoe needs to convey a sense of moral reality. After all, pot making, interesting as it may be, gains in fascination if making becomes an expression of personality. Finally, the Horatian tradition of which Defoe was a product amply justifies his thinking of narrative seriousness as something to be invented apart from the episodic flux and added to it, both for its didactic value and as a way to give at least the impression of form. Earlier narrative abounds with instances of clearly separable, often incommensurable, story and moral. From the *Gesta Romanorum*, with its wild and ruthless allegorical applications of the literal details of stories, to the ubiquitous gallows tracts, with their moralizing of every unhappy felon's life, Defoe could look back at a panorama of fiction rendered profitable. Frequently, as the modern reader regards these various attempts to legitimate fabulating, the "morals" extracted seem ultimately to reduce and trivialize the complexity and concreteness of narrative. Perhaps ethical criticism always runs this risk. So perspicuous a critic as Samuel Johnson could seriously argue that, in part, *King Lear* teaches "this important moral, that villany is never at a stop, that crimes lead to crimes, and at last terminate in ruin."[31]

This additive relationship between story and ideology can lead to a certain farrago, a mismatching of person or event with message that is frequently evident in *Robinson Crusoe* and is positively charming in *Moll Flanders*, since Moll moralizes everything and never concludes what the reader expects her to. Yet the activity of mind behind this "matching up" virtually negates possibilities for novelistic potentiality to be realized. Crusoe can look back on his life and see the beginning of his odyssey as somehow figural, but only because Defoe has conceived of moral seriousness as excess but essential baggage. For this reason, the retrospective point of view, as inconsistently as it may operate, is a boon to Defoe. Crusoe can plausibly comment without violating the superficial illusion of historicity. Even so, one should not confuse this attempt to give an imitated true story minimal seriousness with later fusions of ethical elements and story. To a great extent Fielding tells the stories he does, and in the ways he does, because he believed certain things. His novels are structures that make virtues of the beliefs he had in life, although the transference is never neat and easy and the structures themselves subordinate belief to the ends of pleasurable storytelling.

The shape of *Robinson Crusoe*, on the other hand, both formally and ethically, remains amorphous. It seems just another partial formula to argue that "it is not Robinson Crusoe we care about, but the account of his adventures."[32] Yet neither should we see more profundity in this book than Defoe put there, unless, of course, we do so with full awareness that *we* are creating the meaning. While we value the book for the impulses that move it toward fiction, toward revelation of personality, at the same time we delight in its whimsy, its antinovelistic and often confusing intersections of disparate traits with Crusoe's retrospective judgments. In a traditional novel contradictions ideally become chiasmata, directed into coherence and agreement by the strong telic structure. We can validly speak of a failure to achieve an intended unity. But Defoe, at least until *Roxana*, steadily goes on refining the vividness of his narrators and matching that life ever more appropriately to the episodic stream. In *Robinson Crusoe*, the impulse and the development to come are blocked by an obvious reluctance to impose consistency at any level of experience or meaning. Even when Defoe employs what is to become his dominant strategy, the revelation of selfhood, one can see several things going on at once. Crusoe's vitality can be local, brief, and discontinuous. It can be reiterative, as in Crusoe's retrospective view of his "sin," never disappearing with closural finality but at the same time never awaking novelistic expectations of a promised and probable fate.

Frequently Defoe complicates Crusoe, it seems, only for the sake of complication, as in the famous "O Drug" apostrophe. In this episode, Crusoe returns to the wrecked ship for more booty and finds a cache of gold and silver. As he gazes at it, he smiles to himself at the sight of what he rightly recognizes to be worthless to a castaway. He even launches into a grandiose address to the personified "Drug": "Thou art not worth . . . the taking off of the Ground . . . I have no Manner of use for thee, e'en remain where thou art, and go to the Bottom as a Creature whose Life is not worth saving" (p. 57). Up to this point there is no problem. The reader shares Crusoe's sense of the money's absurd inutility, although he may be a bit puzzled, and at the same time amused, by a speech addressed to some coins. In this way does Crusoe *invite* speculation while not strictly *requiring* it. Immediately, however, one is asked to make some sort of judgment, since Crusoe adds: "However, upon Second Thoughts, I took it away."

Almost every critic of the book has fought a few rounds with this passage, but one recent example will serve to point up the central difficulty of interpretation here. Everett Zimmerman notes that irony is the issue, mentioning Ian Watt and William Halewood as two opposed combatants over the question. Zimmerman's analysis is admirable: "If 'irony' means only the recognition of a discrepancy between conduct and statement, temporarily unnoticed by a character, then this passage is ironic: surely both Defoe and his narrator, Crusoe, must be assumed to be aware of the sharply presented contradictions here. But if in a broader sense, it is meant that Defoe designed a structure to expose the failings of Crusoe's whole mode of behavior—failings never fully recognized by the character himself—then it seems to me that the passage is not ironic."[33] Apart from a small difficulty—how can we speak of Crusoe, Defoe's creation, being "aware" of anything except what he tells us—Zimmerman is correct. Translated into my terms, the discrepancy is not novelistically purposeful, and any judgment one makes of Crusoe must of necessity originate not with the text but (as with my puzzlement over why Crusoe speaks to the money) with one's private associations.

Zimmerman, however, wants this situation to signify even more than he perhaps realizes, for he has just previously argued that "we are accustomed by this time to see a conflict between Crusoe's abstractions and his actions." He then adds that our "confidence that he will not leave the money behind results in part from our faith in consistency of character."[34] Here is a contradiction. The sort of tacit knowledge Zimmerman speaks of can result only if there indeed exists a "structure" of implication. Yet most readers, including one as sensitive as Coleridge, indicate that their response to the passage is a kind of surprised wonder. To fit Zimmerman's dialectic of abstraction and action, Crusoe's behavior *must* be interpreted, else there is no explanatory force to his hypothesis. This is the sort of thing semantic, analogical criticism can do to one's tacit, matter-of-fact experience of narrative. If we resist the temptation to analogize this passage—and there is no reason to do so except to find out what a more stubbornly literal interpretation might uncover—we shall see that the appropriate response to Crusoe's about-face is indeed "unpinned" fascination. That is, *no* interpretation of it is called for, or, indeed, ruled out: one may respond to it in various personal fashions. The question of the passage's meaning only comes up because literary history and not the book's structure teaches us that the whole is a novel. The "confidence" Zimmerman feels is a kind of wishful thinking born of private associations.

This is not to say that our bemused state destroys our pleasure. Quite the contrary, the reader's fascination—and Defoe's advance over much previous narrative—results from Defoe's ability to collect as many of such moments as he can. The desire to refine the presentation of idiosyncratic personality within an overall illusion of factuality led to many such crossings of traits and events, powerful by virtue of their very equivocation. As Rader has said of Moll, life is just one damn thing after another; at least, life would exhibit Defoe's kind of vagaries if it were "epitomized." What has not yet been understood is how unnovelistic such unfixed confusion is. Rader is the only modern critic to insist that the mechanics of factual replication virtually preclude the traditional novel, a form whose standard of taste deplores loose ends, no matter how many may dangle in any example of the form. In addition, the discontinuities of *Robinson Crusoe* are not limited to the presentation of the narrator's personality. Those lines in which Defoe tries to link with some causal force traits and actions also fail to lead to anything but formal confusion, although his attempts constitute an important step in creating novelistic possibilities. While mere linkage does not imply necessary connection, if an author bent on stringing together episodes happens to hit upon one that, by some internal geometry of its own, allows action, character, and thought to be related necessarily rather than casually, then probability can arise unbidden. Such a possibility, developed fully by Defoe at the end of *Roxana*, suggests how the novel might come about, as well as how it might fall into disrepute. Aside from requiring firm and predictable closure and completeness, the traditional action implies a belief in order, and neither finality nor neatness are greatly admired today.

Yet for this fusion to occur, even adventitiously, the portrayal of events and personality cannot remain a binary operation. A standard of appropriate matching cannot lead to causality. For instance, the difference between Crusoe's world and Macbeth's is in part this: Crusoe *can* be whatever the episode demands—fearless, timid, resourceful, at a loss, and so on—within fairly wide limits of consistency; Macbeth *must* be what his sequence requires, although it is not a matter of congruence but radical contradiction. The Macbeth that Malcolm and Macduff seek to destroy is indeed a "dead butcher." Even so, the task of every spectator or reader of the play is to reconcile that Macbeth with the vastly different one whose own actions have filled him with horror and disgust. This is inconsistency only apart from Shakespeare's plot, which harmonizes the radical contradiction and subordinates it fully to the end of creating pity for a man who, seen only from the outside, would elicit only those emotions proper to punitive tragedy. The achievement of *Roxana* is the discovery of a relationship of necessity. In *Robinson Crusoe* there is frequently not only no fusion of personality with the other elements of the story, there is no purposeful contradiction. To choose between the Crusoe who has enchanted children with his mastery of obdurate nature and the Crusoe who, Jonah-like, flees but then finds his God is an unnecessary task. He is both, but not in the same way that Macbeth is both the "confident tyrant" and the man who realizes that to know his deed, "'twere best not know" himself. Crusoe's various selves often coalesce, but only as a result of the loosest juxtaposition. From his father's admonitions, from his first captain's prophetic outburst that he "would not set . . . Foot in the same Ship" with Crusoe again "for a Thousand Pounds" (p. 15), the reader can easily accept the narrator's judgment that he set sail in an "ill Hour" (p. 7). The storm, his illness, and his subsequent shipwreck, not to mention his later being taken by pirates, should have convinced him his place was on dry land. Yet there is never more than the scantest probability that

Crusoe will return to that "best State in the World . . . the upper Station of *Low Life*" his father had wished him to accept (p. 4). Crusoe's retrospective lamentations about his own foolishness never prevent the reader from desiring that he again set out to seek his fate; this lack of apprehension clearly indicates that this is an additive and not a progressive pattern.

If *Robinson Crusoe* were indeed a coherent negative example of the sinfulness of disobedience, as many, including Crusoe himself, have claimed, then it either fails or, as Stanley Fish says of *Paradise Lost*, confirms the reader in his own sinfulness, since the ostensible use of the story is contradicted by how one experiences it.[35] At the very least, one's pleasure in the fruits of Crusoe's disobedience would then be an unintended consequence of Defoe's moral aims.[36] It is a curious hypothesis that converts what for many readers has been the book's principal charm into an incidental and slightly illicit side issue to the "real" meaning, be it spiritual or economic. The operation most of Defoe calls for is not the active acquiescence the novel demands but rather passive acceptance; unlike the traditional novelist, Defoe molds no positive community of shared value. One can recognize the validity of Crusoe's belief that his desire for travel was an "evil influence" in his life without abstracting the proposition from the concrete local context that lends it experiential appropriateness. Moreover, one's minimal acceptance of appropriateness generates no strong expectations. Given Crusoe's years of privation, one can see the rightness of his views without turning them into some kind of ontological absolute. Crusoe's experience, not his rhetoric, is the "message" of the book, otherwise readers would never wish so strongly that he set back out again at any time he has achieved mundane security.

In the brief episode of Crusoe's career as a Brazilian planter, for example, Defoe had a situation of capitalistic activity he would later successfully exploit in *Colonel Jack*. Here he hurries over it in a few pages. The two years Crusoe struggles for subsistence occupy one sentence. In such situations the narrator at his obtrusive best steps forward to point out how foolish his younger self was: "Had I continued in the Station I was now in, I had room for all the happy things to have yet befallen me, for which my Father so earnestly recommended a quiet retired Life, and of which he had so sensibly describ'd the middle Station of Life to be full of; but other things attended me, and I was still to be the wilful Agent of all my own Miseries" (p. 38). As Crusoe recognizes, the retired life is "an Employment quite remote" to his "Genius," and if he had remained a planter he "might as well ha' staid at Home" (p. 35). Instead of a complex drama of sin, retribution, and repentance, there is a minimally coherent, iterative pattern in which certain choices—returning home, settling down—have arbitrarily been precluded by Crusoe's "Genius." Many readers will agree with Crusoe when he says that going to sea again "was the most preposterous Thing that ever Man in such Circumstances could be guilty of" (p. 40). Since he knows what the consequences were, he must be right, but now, Crusoe, get on with the story. If anything, the retrospective rumblings of doom whet the reader's appetite, but not in the same way, for example, as does Oedipus's accusing Tiresias of having sold his services to Creon. Sophocles' entire plot cooperates in establishing this as the moment when Oedipus learns about his own destruction, and we anticipate the revelation with dread. Crusoe's next adventure, it is known from the ones past, will be interesting; but there is no way of predicting what its effect will be. Until he reaches the island, Crusoe's retrospection serves primarily as a storytelling device and as a kind of shorthand way of adding an illusion of moral seriousness.

Once he is on the island, the relationship between Crusoe's spirituality and his quotidian surroundings changes slightly, in part because Defoe then no longer needs to motivate episodic progression quite so artificially. Crusoe's reflections on his God seem less gratuitous when they occur in the immediate context of solitude and issue from the younger Crusoe. The situation of exile, even the peace that comes from his mastering of nature, might seem less than ideal as a scene for the agonies of repentance, but there is nothing inappropriate about showing Crusoe repent and thrive. Neither is there any sustained attempt to establish a causal connection between Crusoe's new relationship with his God and his quotidian activities on the island. Such a pattern, comprising as it might a sort of comedy of divine reward, is not what Defoe has in mind. Crusoe has displayed his resourcefulness from the start. He does not repent as a result of discovering his place in the cosmos, nor does he find that place after repenting. As with his "Genius," the justification for events is that they occur: he falls ill, has a dream, and discovers that he has not been paying enough attention to God. There is causality here, but of a very simple sort not dependent on character, much less profound self-discovery or change. Crusoe's repentance is a convenient *topos*. Roxana lives a life of sin, desires to conceal that life, and as a result falls into complicity in the death of a daughter who wants to reveal her, a girl Roxana would prefer to love rather than murder. Roxana is doomed by her own character, by what she has learned to desire and fear, by the very perils of choice itself. Between the two ways of telling a story is an ethical chasm that will have to be examined later.

Crusoe's religious reflections and his conduct in regard to them are impeachable only if one holds novelistic standards over them. During his illness he takes "a leisurely View of the Miseries of Death," which leads him to "reproach" himself with his "past Life," one of such "uncommon Wickedness" that he has "provok'd the Justice of God" (p. 90). Having Crusoe dream of an avenging angel, angry at Crusoe's inability to accept the "Blessing" of a "happy and easy" way of life—as Crusoe interprets the message—conveniently and effectively establishes a climate for repentance. Even so, the necessity to repent, the past transgressions for which his soul has sickened, have not been sufficiently represented—but only by novelistic standards. If few readers ever ponder just what Crusoe sees as so sinful in his past, it is only because Defoe has chosen a narrative strategy that does not call for the implicatory depth of conduct and linkage between choice and fate that the novel often demands, that even Roxana's story will require. Perhaps in the Puritan view repentance need involve neither spectacular misdeeds nor a marked change in behavior subsequent to repenting. Even so, this is only to suggest that the Puritan view of man and his relationship to his God may not be especially promising as novelistic material. George Starr concludes that the spiritual overlay of Crusoe's story disappears from the later narratives. As Defoe becomes more interested in representing personality, and more skillful at it, he gradually ceases to be concerned about the didactic use of his narrators—although he continues to argue for the instructional value of his stories in prefaces, and his narrators, like Moll, moralize their experiences—and stops worrying about the illusion of factuality, which he initially felt had to be maintained. The discontinuity that some analytical readers, for whom Defoe was not writing, feel between Crusoe's actions and his spirituality, and between his view of the seriousness of his "sin" and an objective judgment of it, is finally neither an intended consequence of Defoe's aims nor a failing of novelistic skill. It is an inadvertent result of an attempt to endow a pseudofactual story with ethical seriousness. Once Defoe is faced, in *Robinson Crusoe*, with a situation that demands that he narratively "justify" Crusoe's conduct, he departs from this older strategy and attempts a novelistic solution.

Character: Potentialities

Crusoe has finally come to terms with both nature and his God when the single footprint intrudes as if with demoniac intention to blast his peace. Fear erases all his longstanding calm, he intends to level his enclosures, drive off his livestock, and destroy his crops in order to conceal his presence. Yet two years pass before he happens upon the grisly evidence of a cannibal feast and he first contemplates destroying "some of these Monsters in their cruel bloody Entertainment" (p. 168). In two or three months of futile watchfulness he comes to reconsider his "outragious" design and begins "with cooler and calmer Thoughts to consider" what he "was going to engage in" (p. 170). Horrid as the savage rites are, the natives "were not Murtherers in the Sense" Crusoe "had before condemn'd them"

58

(p. 171). Nor have they directly threatened him. With the coalescence of moral and practical scruples, he comes to a "kind of Full-stop," seeing his design, since "Religion joyn'd in," as "no less a Sin, than that of wilful Murther" (pp. 172–173). For a year he plays the sentinel no more, but the experience has changed his life and filled him with new concerns.

When the cannibals chance to land on his side of the island, Crusoe's mind changes again. The macabre remains of a feast elicit both righteous anger and a desire to act, so that he passes fifteen months in a "murthering Humour" (p. 184). As if by accident Defoe has established a novelistic situation, in which significant choice rests not just on the dictates of Crusoe's "Genius" but also on the exigencies of the situation modified by ethical issues arising complexly from it. His "Perturbation of . . . Mind" establishes a tension, a need to act so that fear many be calmed (p. 185). Yet any sort of direct action would involve killing, something Crusoe has already decided would be wrong. What is clearly necessary, before this "very strange Encounter" takes place, is the full representation of Crusoe's anxiety so that his conduct reveals its ethical dimension and, at the same time, some narrative justification, apart from the clichés of casuistry, for what he is about to do. Ethical concerns dictate that episodic motivation be powerful.

The birth of the novel does not date from this moment, but the result is a shift from personage to something like novelistic character. In this episode at least, Defoe has a standard of specification that has risen internally. That Defoe "must" do something at this point in the sequence also implies another rarity, if the sequence is examined from a reader's viewpoint: Defoe has now created something like what Wayne Booth calls an implied author, an ordering power behind the flow of events.[37] Once Crusoe must be this and not that, once his personality can no longer freely float, the reader perceives design and a probable outcome, a definite departure from Defoe's ordinary randomness. Neither Crusoe's fear nor his indignation justifies his killing twenty men, as he properly concludes. So Defoe interjects a seemingly digressive episode that can be used, owing to the virtues of narrative, as a rhetorical explanation for what Crusoe is about to do. In the midst of his concern about the savages, a ship founders off the coast of his island. Defoe needs this episode because the novelistic instability of Crusoe's fear and his opposing need to act could potentially last indefinitely. There is nothing *within* Crusoe that would allow for plausible completion of the sequence. Indeed, it is Defoe's usual practice to allow vital conflict to dissipate gradually without strong closure. In this case, Crusoe's discovery that the ship is empty, when he had so fervently hoped for some companions at last, plunges him into despair. His yearnings for human contact, thrown into the scales, provide the justification necessary to resolve the instability with probability and a degree of ethical decorum. "One Fellow-Creature . . . to have convers'd with," Crusoe laments after he sees that the ship is not anchored but stuck on a reef: "In all the time of my solitary Life, I never felt . . . so strong a Desire after the Society of my Fellow-Creatures, or so deep a Regret at the want of it" (p. 188). So important is this justification to the novelistic subsequence that, in what is rare for him, Defoe mirrors, with gestural equivalents, his narrator's inner turmoil: "I believe I repeated the Words, *O that it had been but One!* A thousand Times; and the Desires were so mov'd by it, that when I spoke the Words, my Hands would clinch together, and my Fingers press the Palms of my Hands, that if I had had any soft Thing in my Hand, it wou'd have crusht it involuntarily; and my Teeth in my Head wou'd strike together, and set against one another so strong, that for some time I cou'd not part them again" (p. 188). Two more years pass and thoughts of escape fill his mind. In his dream of rescuing one of the cannibals' victims, fear and loneliness unite with the long-suppressed desire to escape this solitary "paradise" and Crusoe wakes into "a very great Dejection of Spirit" (p. 199). Yet his desires still conflict with his old scruples against killing and it is a "great while" before he can "reconcile" himself to the certain carnage. Finally, "Desire of Deliverance at length master'd all the rest"; the subsequent year's delay only makes him more "eager" (p. 200).

I have examined this sequence at such length and in such detail because, unlike most episodes in *Robinson Crusoe*, here content and order of representation do matter greatly. An instability has been endowed with a degree of probability. Seemingly unrelated events have been subsumed by a kind of local teleology; a pattern exists, requiring certain judgments. Indeed, it is only at such points that narrative sequences can impose their wills on a reader. The faint voice of the novel-to-come is heard. For example, when the cannibals land with their captives, Crusoe perceives that he is "call'd plainly by Providence to save this poor Creature's Life" (p. 202), a bit of casuistry one need not stumble over, since the most compelling justification for his actions has already come from the carefully revealed psychological progression. As Tillyard remarked, "This slow timing is very remarkable in Defoe, who elsewhere tends to crowd his events thick, and it adds incalculably to the dignity of what happens on the island."[38] "Dignity," resulting from what I have called justification, arises only at those moments of approach to novelistic character. The pattern acquires forward movement, structural purposefulness that sweeps away possible ethical objections. We acquiesce, or at least the logic of the progression asks for our cooperation; the pattern attempts to impose its values on us, diminishing ambiguity. If we resist its blandishments, we know our willful substitution of our own beliefs somehow ignores an implicit formal request. While most of the time one is free to judge Crusoe, and most of Defoe's other narrators, as one chooses, here the sequence requires definite belief, as a condition of its very existence as a dynamic instability. Defoe has found a dramatic method of imposing his beliefs on a reader, if only in one section of one story.

Crusoe gains his "Fellow-Creature," Friday, but the killing necessary to do so does not convert Crusoe into a bloodthirsty racist. Defoe's careful preparation was intended to forestall such a judgment. Even so, Defoe cannot find a way, in this book, to continue the complex relationship of elements that led to narrative justification. It is as if the standards of constructing pseudofactual stories dictate that potentially novelistic sequences always be shunned or quickly ended if they rise by accident from the imaginative unconscious. At any rate, Defoe expends no effort in justifying the later slaughter of twenty-one more cannibals. His neat little ledgerlike account, in which he has Crusoe list how each savage was dispatched, reveals an author who has ceased to think novelistically. This is a return to a narrative world in which personality is free to pursue, with minimal consistency, its own vagaries. That it would be difficult to reconcile the yearning Crusoe with the later bloodthirsty one, except with some self-confirming theory of "irony," only indicates that it is Defoe's *way* of telling his stories that frequently shifts; he does not in general tell stories based on dynamic change itself. There will be other substructures in which novelistic potentiality resides, but until *Roxana*, Defoe prefers not to develop those new possibilities.

Fact, Fiction, and the Reader

Defoe wrote for readers who affirmed an absolute and perhaps un-bridgeable chasm between fact and fiction, history and deception, at least in narrative. The idea of a "nonfiction novel" would have struck them prima facie as ludicrous equivocation.[39] Earlier critics in the Horatian tradition, like Sidney, had skirted the problem neatly by stressing the moral efficacy of poetry while insisting that the poet "nothing affirms, and therefore never lieth." A century later, Dominique Bouhours could argue that "there is a great deal of difference between fiction and falsehood" because "in truth, the fabulous world, which is the world of poets, has nothing real in it."[40] Even so, the vast number of fabricated "memoirs" and "true histories," some appearing even while Bouhours wrote, indicate that most readers operated under quite a different set of rules, stemming, as Philip Stewart says, from the "implicit syllogism that fiction, being invented, is untrue; being untrue, it is manifestly the opposite of truth: it therefore has all the moral probity of a lie."[41] Novak has concluded that "Defoe's insistence on the truth of his fictions is frequently ambiguous." The evidence reads otherwise.[42] If there is any ambiguity, it is because Defoe, like his narrators, is rhetorically slippery. In the preface to *Colonel Jack*, Defoe says, *"neither is it of the least Moment to enquire whether the Colonel hath told his own Story true or not; If he has made a* History *or a* Parable, *it will be equally useful."*[43] Novak finds equivocation over the question of whether this be history or parable. But the quandary disappears when one notes the unambiguous pose that Jack is himself the storyteller, an assertion backed up by the book's internal strategies of illusion.

By 1722, when *Colonel Jack* appeared, Defoe probably felt secure enough in the reception of his narratives not to worry about cries of romance. Defoe was by then writing recognizable fictions, if not novels, as well as imitations of true stories like the *Journal*, which has such a solid illusion of truth that Defoe did not even bother with a confirmatory preface. Yet a problem remains. To some extent Defoe always expects his stories to be taken as true, even those in which the evidence is ambiguous because the pleasures of autobiography have been refined into a kind of artful principle. The illusion of referentiality, that out there somewhere in the countryside sits a real Crusoe inditing his memoirs, may often be more or less undermined by fictional tendencies. Even so, unless one is willing to entertain seriously the possibility that Defoe was only the editor of all these memoirs, then the illusion remains just a skillful "trick." For one ingenious critic early in this century, the question did not matter much. Despite Defoe's inventions, for Watson Nicholson *A Journal of the Plague Year* was reliable history.[44] Yet, in spite of attempts to show that history and fiction are not really far apart, readers clearly react to them in very different ways. If the distinction has any validity at all, how can one continue to delight in a book that is known to be fiction, while recognizing at the same time, at least tacitly, that it makes claims for literal credence no novel does? The problem does not go away once it is disclosed, as Starr says, that Defoe distinguished "between wholesome and pernicious falsehoods, and that only the latter should be called lies."[45] Only someone with a decided relish for literary hoaxes would continue to read Boswell's journals if he learned that they were really fabrications of, say, Colonel Isham. Part of a possible solution to the question must be put aside until the next chapter, but for now a few suggestions.

If Defoe had used Crusoe only as an unpersonalized observer, we would not only recognize that he had not advanced significantly over previous pseudohistory, we probably would not be reading the book. The value of *Robinson Crusoe* lies rather in its celebrations of personality and in its occasional shadings over into potentially novelistic effects. Yet the undercutting of the factual illusion by protonovelistic elements, and even by the consistent refining and epitomizing of Crusoe's personality, results in an ongoing conflict of phenomenological evidence. Books ask, even demand, certain operations of us. Walter Wilson declared in 1830 that "the reader reluctantly admits any part" of *Robinson Crusoe* "to be a fiction." One nineteenth-century critic concerned with the process of reading, De Quincey, complicates the matter by noting Defoe's invention of "neutral details" about which there is so little "at all amusing" that "girls" read Defoe's books "for novels" and "men read them for histories."[46] Sexist implications to the side, it may be that this double character can apply not just to different classes of readers but also to single readers at different times. Within the overall illusion of truth, bolstered by those "neutral details," exist situations of patterned fantasy, to which one reacts but cannot make full sense of, which one cannot place within the context of a "true story." Clinging to an older tradition, *Robinson Crusoe* at the same time raises ambiguous claims to novelhood.

Recovering Meaning

Defoe's strategies of presentation, interesting as they may be as signaling the way to the novel, also raise questions about the possibilities for meaning in narrative, insoluble ones if we assume all stories signify, or fail to signify, in the same way. In the past, it has been believed that the question led back to Defoe, to his skill in "judging his material." I have tried to suggest that meaning arises differentially because some ways of relating stories limit, provoke, and even preclude meaning of any determinate sort. It may be that one can never be confident at any time in Defoe that one is employing an appropriate "recovery method," or even that meaning is recoverable. It is not just the passé notion that stories can signify in ways their authors do not dream of. Authors may write stories not intended to mean at all, at least in the expected ways.

The problem stretches beyond Defoe. As soon as one recognizes that interpretative dilemmas with Defoe often stem from refusing to sort out varying intentions and effects, and the relationships, causal or adventitious, between them, then Defoe becomes the problem of the novel. I do not propose to "solve" the difficulty, but I do hope to show that meaning in narrative, as it depends on the storyteller's art, is no simple matter, as Martin Battestin seemed to believe when—commenting on Sheldon Sacks's attempt to discern varying "shapes" of belief in the novel—he confidently remarked that such an inquiry demonstrated a "self-evident premiss."[47] Of course, all novels mean. One lesson Defoe does teach is to look behind the façade of narrative simplicity to find the complex strategies of signification hiding there.

III

The Impersonal Narrator

EVEN WITH ITS NOVELISTIC POSSIBILITIES, the episode of Crusoe's yearnings for escape and subsequent action issued from a reluctant imagination. Defoe's ability to control Crusoe's personality, to subdue it to something more than locally purposeful, becomes most apparent in such sequences. He becomes a manipulator, to some extent controlling the possibilities for his reader's experience with the story. Yet such episodes were artistic accidents, fortuitous aberrations that threaten the integrity of the factual pose. Invention masquerading as fact always risks discovery by analytical readers, ones like Charles Gildon, for example, who immediately dubbed *Robinson Crusoe* a mere romance. The illusion remains secure only so long as the author remains identical to the narrator in the reader's apprehension. That earlier impersonators like Courtilz did not have to learn that lesson only suggests that within them fiction and literal truth did not struggle quite so mightily as they did within Defoe.

At the same time that Defoe had discovered the dangers of letting his imagination take over a factual sequence, he had found out how to prevent it from happening. Crusoe seems most historical, most like an uninvented reporter, when he merely observes, plodding his dull, impersonal way through a succession of "farther adventures" tied together only by his insubstantial presence. After Crusoe, then,

Defoe faced two broad choices of how to proceed. He could continue in the older tradition of replicating the effects of true stories, at the same time attempting to incorporate subjects of more enduring interest. Or he could set out for a kind of narrative terra incognita involving the pursuit of imaginative effects, even at the cost of destroying the historical referentiality he thought narrative storytelling demanded. Defoe actually follows both paths, but I shall examine only the first in this chapter.

The Insipidity of Truth

The more radically innovative possibilities of *Robinson Crusoe* did not become clear to Defoe as quickly as did more traditional ones. Familiar as he was with a great number of fabricated memoirs and "true histories," whether knowing them as inventions or not, he must have realized that a narrative with a convincing factual power could also be made interesting. Within a few months of the gratifying success of *Robinson Crusoe*—four editions in little over three months—Defoe set Crusoe out again in the *Farther Adventures*. Having stumbled upon a situation on Crusoe's island that occasionally shifted elements toward fictive possibilities, Defoe now will allow no such marring intrusions. This was to be a road show, appropriately fixed out with a "Map of the World, in which is Delineated the Voyages of Robinson Crusoe."[1] No study of human isolation, enlivened with inapt juxtapositions of trait and event, Defoe's sequel manages to avoid all such complications in order to maintain its factual integrity. This second Crusoe owes his being to the pre-island episodes of the first part: the narrator is a retailer of wonders and exotica, only slightly more humanized than any veritable reporter of his travel experiences, like Woodes Rogers. By avoiding the concentrated imaginative force of Crusoe's interactive personality, Defoe advanced in the art of hiding his tracks, but only at the cost of revealing the insipidity of truth that feigned history can lead to.

The *Farther Adventures* indicates that Defoe did not recognize his own secret of success. True, it would have been cruel and unusual punishment to have dropped a superannuated Crusoe down on some deserted sandspit and forced him, perhaps without benefit of fortuitous plunder, to create another Little England in the wilderness. Even so, Defoe ought to have had little difficulty in creating situations in which fascinating personality predominated over a mere succession of events. It is almost as if the spatial confines of the island were all that made Crusoe's vividness possible. At any rate, the resurrected narrator seldom rises above the clichés of inner life: "I must confess I was now very uneasy, and thought myself, including the late escape from the longboats, to have been in the most dangerous condition that I was in through all my past life; for whatever ill circumstance I had been in, I was never pursued for a thief before; nor had I ever done anything that merited the name dishonest" (p. 226). Here is Defoe's usual method: find a *topos* and fill it. Aside from the interesting detail—for literary history, that is—of Crusoe's never having been "pursued for a thief before," this passage is notable for what has disappeared from Crusoe's portrayal. Nowhere, for example, is there anything like the kinesthetic intensity of the earlier Crusoe: "I walk'd about on the Shore, lifting up my Hands . . . wrapt up in the Contemplation of my Deliverance, making a Thousand Gestures . . . reflecting upon all my Comerades that were drown'd" (p. 46). To employ a geological analogy, the successive concretions of Crusoe's personality, resulting in a certain complex richness, have yielded to a monogenetic method. Crusoe is imagined whole in the second part, but only as a reportorial device. Even Defoe's language, never a model of concision, indicates that there is some truth to Gildon's charge that Defoe intends to "swell the bulk . . . up to a five Shilling Book": "Been in . . . was in . . . been in."[2]

It is not always obvious to authors why a best-seller has succeeded. So one need not be too surprised that Defoe turned, in his sequel, directly to the *least* promising mode of storytelling he had unearthed. Another partial explanation is indeed Charles Gildon, to whose parody of *Robinson Crusoe* I have already alluded. Paul Dottin contends, on evidence he does not cite, that this satiric mocking "annoyed De Foe very much."[3] Since it came out after the *Farther Adventures*, it would not have been the proximate cause of Defoe's retreat from fictive possibilities, unless rumors of what Gildon was doing reached Defoe before Gildon published. Gildon's intention, executed with the characteristic asperity that was finally to land him in *The Dunciad*, was to point out two main orders of failing: simple errors and oversights, failings of specific knowledge; and inconsistency of portrayal. In his preface to the *Farther Adventures*, Defoe indicates that someone had already chided him about the obvious qualities of romance in the first part, but he boasts of his "triumph" in refuting that charge and another, that he has been guilty of "errors in geography." Such cavils, crows Defoe, "have proved abortive," and literary history has by and large proved him correct. Gildon counters, however, that "all but the very *Canaille* are satisfied" by such blunders "of the Worthlessness of the Performance."[4] Although most readers do not find such errors disturbing, or even notice them most of the time, they prove to Gildon that the book is a counterfeit: Crusoe stuffs his pockets with bread, Defoe having forgotten that his hero had doffed his breeches to swim to the ship; Crusoe goes for pen and ink when he had long ago run out.

Gildon's objections, of this first sort at least, show us how Augustans thought of probability, and how quick they could be to point out violations of it. For Aristotle, literary likelihood meant an internal system of relations, not necessarily correspondent with what one thinks is even possible in the real world. By Gildon's time, probability meant how any literary sequence measured up to the *comment c'est* of life. What for Aristotle were errors not "in the essentials of the poetic art," for example, "to make the horse in movement have both right legs thrown forward" (*Poetics* 25), became damning evidence of ignorance or, worse, in a work that pretended to be literally true, a clear indication of fiction. On this basis Gildon attacks Defoe in the mock dialogue between "Dan" and his creations, Friday and Crusoe. Friday complains of Defoe's linguistic half-learning: "Have injure me, to make me such Blockhead, so much contradiction, as to be able to speak *English tolerably well* in a Month or two, and not to speak it better in twelve Years after; to make me go out to be kill'd by the Savages, only to be a Spokesman to them, tho' I did not know, whether they understood one Word of my Language."[5]

With this last complaint, Gildon slides perceptibly toward pinpointing Defoe's very real problems in portraying Crusoe. For example, Gildon has *his* Crusoe complain to Defoe that he resents being "made" into a "strange whimsical, inconsistent Being . . . extravagantly Zealous, and as extravagantly Remiss." Now this is a different order of objection from the first one, in that it seems to suggest an internal standard of useful fictionality. Elsewhere Gildon confirms that this is what he has in mind, as when he argues that Crusoe's "Moral Reflections" are "in many Places of no manner of Relation to the Occasion on which they are deliver'd," a charge as easily leveled against Moll's "serious inferences." Gildon could not talk about *Robinson Crusoe* in this manner unless the factual illusion had broken down for him, either through the failure of consistency mentioned earlier, or because of more positive but ambiguous evidence of fictionality. Veracious narrative does not call for judgments of probability, history not being a matter of likelihood, except in instances where the historian lacks information or has faltered—and Crusoe reports his own history. Gildon, nevertheless, insists on interpreting what in a successful factual illusion would simply demand acceptance as human anomaly: "to render any *Fable* worthy of being receiv'd into the Number of those which are truly valuable, it must *naturally* produce in its Event some useful Moral, either *express'd* or *understood*" (my emphasis).[6] Successful fabulating requires the coherent communication of beliefs, their yoking to the representation of character and event in a probable manner.

This was all good fun, and of course Defoe had the profits from *Robinson Crusoe* to reassure him he had done something right. But as overstated as Gildon's rhetoric was, his basic objections might have unsettled an author who, at this point at least, saw his success in terms of creating undetectable illusion, seeming "true history."

Clearly Defoe's activities after *Robinson Crusoe*, including the *Farther Adventures*, indicate that he is in search of strategies of internal confirmation that would fool even a Gildon, even if at the same time they take Defoe away from the qualities of narrative which in fact had made his first effort a success. In the following year he writes "lives," "histories," and "accounts," but nothing, with the exception of parts of *Captain Singleton*, that approaches the symbiosis of Crusoe and his island. There are also more or less "straight" biographies: a *Life* of Baron de Goertz (advertised July 13, 1719); a *Faithful . . . Account* of Dickory Cronke, the famous "Dumb Philosopher" (October 13); an *Account* of the *Enterprises of Captain Avery* (December 10); a *History . . . of Mr. Duncan Campbell* (April 30, 1720); and a *History of the Wars, of . . . Charles XII* (May 24). If Defoe invented any details in these journalistic narratives, they hardly would be detectable without external contradiction, so firmly does Defoe establish a sense of referentiality.

Yet *Singleton* indicates that Defoe could not refrain entirely from inventing stories. Other than the attempts to "moralize" *Robinson Crusoe*—and thereby sidestep Gildon—with the *Serious Reflections*, 1720 stands out chiefly because of the *Memoirs of a Cavalier*. Defoe's main task here was almost the opposite of what it would be in *Moll Flanders*. Defoe takes public events and designs a narrator who serves as both witness and confirmer of truth. History controls the point of view, subdues the emotional force when personality interacts with events, and even makes possible the referential significance of the account. Defoe's reasons for writing such a book are fairly obvious. The residue of unrest remaining from the Jacobite scare of "the '15" would assure interest in a personal history of the Civil War. The Thirty Years' War was a bit more distant but, as James T. Boulton suggests, the death in 1718 of Charles XII, grandnephew of Gustavus Adolphus, guaranteed that an account of the warrior-king would attract some readers, even if only those devotees of military history. All that remained was for Defoe to redact available accounts of both wars, carefully observing chronology and geography, and the intrinsic interest of war reported at first hand would ensure success. As Malcolm J. Bosse notes, Defoe's intention seems to have been to maintain "a high level of intensity for this story by refusing to vary it with domestic or romantic matters."[7] Intensity, however, is precisely what Defoe fails to achieve, in large part because the limitations on subject matter and, especially, on the role of the narrator, lead to a successful illusion, but also to a blandness and monotony virtually precluding the exploration of complex narrative situations.

The paring down of his material, necessary perhaps for his intention to succeed, results in an avoidance of the variety constituting his chief mode of refinement later on. One effective strategy that arises from this intention is what might be called "anticlimactic omission": induce the reader to expect the report of a great, perhaps pivotal, battle, then invent a reason why the narrator could not quite get to the scene on time. If enough battle action has been narrated already, the reader will not be overly frustrated and will conclude that this account has to be true, else why would anyone be so tiresome? Just before the decisive battle of the Civil War, the Cavalier asks leave of the king to "go by *Shrewsbury*" to visit his father, "the most Unsoldier-like" shirking of his duty he was ever "guilty of" (p. 256). Missing the last action leaves him "disconsolate" and the reader frustrated, although the balk is less annoying for the knowledge that this all must be true. Otherwise, why would any fabulator spurn the chance to recreate one of the most important events in recent English history? Earlier in the book, the Cavalier had mentioned the Duke of Bavaria's "Chamber of Rarities," automatically stirring interest just by the phrase. He then offhandedly reports, "I expected to have staid here some Time, and to have taken a very exact Account of this curious Laboratory; but being commanded away, I had not Time" (p. 97). Defoe has Crusoe do what looks like this same sort of thing, as when Crusoe tantalizingly mentions that he once thought to brew some beer. The difference of course is that in any of Defoe's epitomes of personality, such omissions contribute additional complexity and allusivity to the portrayal. With the Cavalier, the interest, if the narrator had not been forestalled in his report, inheres in the unseen events or sights. As De Quincey once remarked of the *Memoirs*, which he called one of Defoe's "poorest forgeries," "as there is nothing at all amusing, we conclude that the author could have no reason to detain us with such particulars but simply because they were true."[8]

Defoe also had to prevent his narrator from drawing the reader into any sort of imaginative empathy. This strategy is not solely a feature of pseudofactual narrative. Hemingway, for example, knew exactly how to divert attention away from the consciousness of characters who, like Nick in "The Killers," serve as devices of the "telling" rather than as elements of the "essence."[9] It may be true, as John R. Searle says, that there "is no textual property, syntactical or semantic, that will identify a text as a work of fiction."[10] Yet the more highly structured a narrative sequence, the more one will tend to respond to it as one does to the complexly implicatory traditional novel. It is this paradox that allows some critics, who very well know Boswell's *Life of Johnson* is not fiction, to talk about it nevertheless as if it had "novelistic" structure.[11] The traditional novel is an affective as well as formal whole: one's knowledge of the probable outcome of a sequence is in part a function of the dynamic interplay between one's desires for a character and one's expectations about what that character's fate will be. In real diaries, few of which have novelistic structures, a reader's feelings of whatever sort are accidents of the humanly believable situation, and not forged consequences of a rapport involving reader, character, and author. What one feels about the Cavalier at any point depends, therefore, on what personal associations one has with the reported events and how much significance one wishes to read into his reportorial role. Disagreements about the Cavalier have for these reasons been different from those about Moll or Crusoe: here the question seems to be not moral but ontological. Secord argues that the memoirs of both the Cavalier and Carleton reveal "nothing of the inner lives of their heroes." Dottin contends that the *Memoirs* fail because of the narrator, the public

73

being "too little impressed with this long-drawn-out succession of military maneuvers, described by a dull and lifeless individual." Novak sees the Cavalier as "hardly more than a narrative device for a description of the religious wars of the seventeenth century." Yet William Trent can somehow perceive "a great artistic advance upon the *History of the Wars of Charles XII*," and Moore can argue that "from the day of his arrival at Calais" the Cavalier "is almost as real a man as Robinson Crusoe." Boulton goes farther: "the Cavalier is no mere pasteboard figure. He is an independent, vital character." More recently, Zimmerman has managed to ride the fence: "the somewhat intermittently presented central character is nevertheless extensively developed."[12] The seeming disagreement arises from a desire to construe the *Memoirs* in different ways, a strong temptation if a work refuses to enforce moral norms; if one insists, for example, on treating it as a novel, and one defines the novel as coherent meaning, then one will want to argue that the Cavalier contributes a significant measure to the overall message of the book. Yet, in absolute terms, the opaque historicity of the book refuses to project a coherent ideology on to the Cavalier's experience. Even the terms critics use hint at the problem. The use of "artistic advance," "independent, vital character," and the term that above all others most effectively stifles inquiry, "real," signals that these are approximate labels for inchoate feelings, instead of formal explanations for affective response.

There are, for example, significantly fewer first-person-singular references in the *Memoirs* than in *Robinson Crusoe*, or in any of Defoe's other memoir "epitomes." Just as in Crusoe's ramblings after the island, the scenic overview and the use of the choric "we" serve to direct attention away from the narrator and place it on events and sights. As a general rule of first-person narration, any shift away from the "I" attenuates whatever sense of personality has emerged. Here then is the literal source of the Cavalier's "thinness." Yet if a critic, for the sake of his thesis, prefers to assimilate the *Memoirs* to Defoe's development as a communicating novelist, he can always do so by generalizing the Cavalier's personality from what is objectively a much smaller quantity of evidence than what Defoe usually provides. Indeed, the Cavalier was not conceived in stone. Boulton ennumerates as evidence of the Cavalier's "vital character" traits such as "shrewd common sense, courage (although also a capacity for fear), initiative, loyalty, and gratitude, concern for others, pragmatic intelligence, and devotion to principle."[13] There is no doubt that the Cavalier has all these virtues; Gulliver has many of them too, and so does Colonel Jack. The difference is one of use. Gulliver's traits are revealed to facilitate satiric attack. He can be insightful and superior to the Lilliputians because the minuscule race's faults and perversities parallel those of Western society; he can be imperceptive and inferior to the Brobdingnagian king because then Gulliver himself is the satiric foil. No one demands any more consistency of Gulliver than his role requires. But then, few would call his book a novel. Colonel Jack lives for a different reason, so that the fascinating reciprocity of person and surroundings may occur. So too Moll. The Cavalier's traits, however, are only on intermittent loan so that he may effectively function reportorially. He is exactly what one would expect a real man intent on events and not himself to be. Viewed from "outside" the illusion, he is what one would expect from a skillful fabricator who does not want his handiwork discovered. The Cavalier must get close enough to military commanders, two of whom happen to be kings, in order to report the inner workings of strategy. He cannot, therefore, be a social pariah like Jack or Singleton. He must remain in the field, so he cannot very well be a coward. His brand of intelligence is exactly the mundane and unimaginative kind necessary in a narrator who must comment on strategy. These literal functions may not be very exciting to someone bent on seeing Defoe and all his work as just another supporting beam in some sort of novelistic macrostructure. Even so, a failure to see that the Cavalier is of the "treatment" while Moll, Jack, Roxana, and, most of the time, Crusoe, are of the "essence" has obscured the concrete problems Defoe had to solve before he could even approach the novel.

If one then grants Defoe's use of the Cavalier as a device, one should also recognize that Defoe's intention therefore includes the possibility that his narrator will seem "lumpish." The book may indeed be "mere historical chronicle," but such it was intended to be.[14] In this line of his storytelling, Defoe is not interested in novelistic effects. He is tailoring his works to an audience who, like Gildon, do not have novelistic tastes or expectations. The impersonality and even the flatness of the Cavalier prevent readers from suspecting that this is just another sensationalist "Secret History" purporting to reveal the private cavorting of public figures. Defoe, that is, even though feigning, observes a certain historical decorum in both his representation and interpretation of events. Like the veritable historian, Defoe must be wary of revolutionary or "revisionist" views, especially of England's own Civil War. One result of Defoe's attention being on events and not personality is that there is much less difficulty determining what Defoe really believed. Since he follows the chronology of events in his sources, he has no need to motivate and vivify episodes by means of the Cavalier's beliefs, as he does with Crusoe; and, since the Cavalier has little life apart from the events, Defoe need develop no complexity in his imaginative conception of him. One escapes thereby the allusivity of a Crusoe or Moll precisely because the Cavalier need possess only the simplest of traits, and not many of those. In such a situation, it is a virtual certainty that the Cavalier's interpretations express at least a large part of what Defoe believes to be the truth. Examples abound in all of Defoe's stories, of course, of ideas he expresses elsewhere. Indeed, some critics seem to think that any idea not explicitly refuted in the story must be endorsed, forgetting as they do that, as Richetti shrewdly writes, "story-telling is by its nature something different from discursive statement."[15] Defoe's presentational strategies conceal sometimes complex relationships of meaning and story, proof that even in pseudofactual narrative significance does not arise in a single manner. In much of Defoe, ascribing every significant idea, expressed or implied, to Defoe himself is simply unwarranted. Not only can one confidently go astray, one certainly obscures whatever fluctuating possibilities for meaning his nascent experiments represent.

The *Memoirs*, and any of his other factual replications, present fewer problems than do his refinements of personality. For instance, the Cavalier's "Aversion to popular Tumults" Defoe expressed as early as 1710: "To raise Tumults, and Riots, is a Method, no People that have their own Safety in View can ever in their Senses think of without Horror."[16] At another point, the Cavalier launches into an encomium on the glories of the *"Swedish* Troops," one that, like so many of the narrator's simple likes and dislikes, neither motivates nor is motivated by any episodic progression (meaning consistently in the *Memoirs* being coordinate and additive, rather than subordinate and causal). Defoe had long before declared his admiration for the "Swedes," in his view "some of the bravest Men in the World."[17] Freed here from the cramp of portraying personality, having no sense of imaginative engagement with his narrator, Defoe's commodious memory supplies opinions out of his journalistic past. Sometimes the ideas reappear virtually unchanged from their previous state. Sometimes the necessities of narration, even in a pseudofactual work like the *Memoirs*, serve, if not to contradict, at least to modify expression or form—rhetorical exigency fostering rhetorical accommodation in a relationship bearing some likeness to the novelistic justification that goes on sporadically in Defoe.

As an example of this modification of views, Defoe long believed that the English had betrayed the Protestant cause when they had failed to assist the Huguenots at La Rochelle in 1628. Indeed, seven English and Dutch ships had actually helped the French defeat the Protestant hero Soubise's fleet in 1625. In 1704, Defoe is careful to exculpate Charles I—he was "ill serv'd," really desired the "Relief of the Protestants," but was practiced upon by the "Managers" of the business. Two years later Defoe has apparently changed his mind, for he accuses Charles of having "rather ruin'd than Assisted" the Huguenots: "He and the *Dutch* lent their ships," and Charles's execution by the Puritans was "God's Judgment" for "Betraying the *Rochellers*."[18] The inculpation could not be less ambiguous. Yet when Defoe comes to write the *Memoirs* fourteen years later he seems to have had third thoughts. The Cavalier observes that when he arrived in France in 1630 the "Protestants were every where disconsolate" over their losses at La Rochelle. They are "without . . . hopes" and a "Protestant Gentleman" tells him that "the *English* had ruined them" by sending, with the Dutch, "Ships to beat" the Huguenots (p. 15). It is insufficient in Defoe's view, however, merely to have a secondary figure assert the interpretation. He devises as a corresponding representational strategy a part for the Cavalier to play in the interchange, in order to impress upon his readers the charge of English duplicity. The Cavalier, surrogate for any reader who cannot bring himself to accept his nation's role in the subjugation of Protestants, "was something startled at the Charge." Even so, his "discourse with this Gentleman" soon convinced him that "the Truth of what he said was undeniable." The "Naval Power of the Protestants" was indeed "unhappily broke by their Brethern of *England* and *Holland*." Defoe has made the point with admirable effectiveness. But what is it? Charles now is mentioned but once, and rather in passing by the "Gentleman." No connection between his actions and his melancholy fate is suggested.

While political rhetoric clearly shapes this brief episode, other pressures bear on it too. Defoe knows in advance, that is, that he will later enlist the Cavalier in the Royalist cause. Having planned out the historical progressions of this account, he can avoid the inconsistency of having a man praise and serve a monarch he had earlier agreed had doomed the French Protestants. He must, that is, maintain Charles as a figure worthy of allegiance. Defoe's general opinion about English treachery and probably his specific one about Charles I remain the same; but the needs of narration dictate a slight muting. Within even the firmest factual illusion resides therefore an everpresent potentiality for ambiguity. Interpretive difficulties can arise whenever the direction of the narrative flow conflicts with even the sincerest of authorial belief. Like the twin faces of a fault, ideology and story abrade in order to accommodate. Sometimes the compromise is an uneasy one, even with a "simple" author like Defoe whose ordinary mode is coordination.

One would not be far wrong to call the special power of the *Memoirs* "historical." In some ways it is only a more skillful version of the political histories he had been writing for a decade. In terms of use, however, there is a narrative world of difference. This is still in the public arena: like the *Short Narrative of . . . Marlborough* (1711), the *Memoirs* treats a subject known in general to all. But while *Marlborough* attempts to mediate issues still important, ones bearing on current policy, the *Memoirs* interprets with historical distance, even though some of the questions, like the fate of European Protestants, may still have had contemporary significance. Defoe has moved from using history, or historical guises, for polemical purposes, to history for its own sake. A generation later, Tom Jones, homeless and friendless, would set out on the road to Scotland, no inner debate necessary to determine that he would fight for his monarch against the invading Pretender. It is doubtful whether, in 1720, very many of Defoe's readers needed any guidance either. Certainly a story in which the narrator manages to give an air of perfect ordinariness about his decision of sides in a civil war would not serve as an effective exemplum. The Cavalier's insouciance directs attention away from personal motivation and toward historical causes and consequences.

The *Memoirs*, then, achieved an advance in the art of concealing art but not an especially propitious one. Factual reconstruction, of the open and avowed or the covert sort, must somehow capture the imagination; the events must be given shape and their profundity revealed. Considered abstractly, as untried material, no moment of history comes prepacked with potential interest. Indeed, once Defoe moves away from public events, he finds ways to endow the daily flux of a Moll's life with far more interest than adventure ever had. Treatment, in true history, feigned history, and fiction, lends the materials of narrative their unique geometries. For this reason, we could never construct a powerful typology of narrative if we looked only at subject. The "what" of narrative tells us little about the "how," about the effects stories can have on readers. In this sense, we cannot say in advance that wars are better subjects for fiction *or* history than are less spectacular events. A battle may yield less as subject matter than a trip in a small boat to a lighthouse. It is a bit misleading, then, to equate Defoe's development with his locating "better" subjects, as Moore does when he compares the *Memoirs* favorably to *Captain Carleton*: "Local guerilla fighters such as the Miguelets were no equal for the gallant Scots in foreign service, and the erratic and amorous Earl of Peterborough was a grotesque substitute for the great Gustavus."[19] One might wonder why an "erratic and amorous" earl would not be superb material, as potential, and, as far as Spanish irregulars, Hemingway did not find them a particularly crippling liability. Actually, neither the *Memoirs* nor *Carleton* have many readers today. They are way stations on the road to the *Journal*.

In the unlikely event the *Memoirs* should ever turn up in Hollywood, the Cavalier's role should be limited to a mere voice-over, a device of linkage. Chronology, geography, and the shadowy diffusion of the narrator would move the viewer from scene to scene. It would not be much of a movie, chronicles not lending themselves well to dramatic presentation. The talents of even a pseudohistorian like Defoe were better turned to events that at least exhibited the artificial unity and compaction provided by limitations of time and place. Thirty Years' wars tend to go on and on. But some events seem to have a unity of their own or can be treated as if they did. In the London Plague of 1665 Defoe found such a subject.

Bestowing Charms on the Monstrous

One recent development in the study of narrative is a belief in the connectedness of fictional narrative with larger structures of meaning, outside any single work, subsuming systems of linguistic praxis or myth from which any story draws at least a part of its significance.

A Journal of the Plague Year would seem to be a perfect example, with its situation of a city beseiged by pestilence and, as it seemed to the narrator, H.F., threatened with annihilation. The possible connections with biblical typology and with classical plague literature suggest a rich allusive potential. Criticism of the book has worked out a number of such illuminating analogies, as in W. Austin Flanders's suggestion that the continuing appeal of the book "cannot lie in the limited formal success of the composition but must be found in its application to the modern reader's experience of life."[20] Although such a view manages to bestow "poetic" significance on a work many have felt was closer to actual history, it does so at the cost of blurring an important distinction, based on one's tacit experience of narratives true and fictional. For Aristotle, poetry was more philosophical than history precisely because the poet dealt in probability. As Samuel Johnson said of Shakespeare, "the event which he represents will not happen, but if it were possible, its effects would be probably such as he has assigned."[21] Yet a close examination of how Defoe conceived of and used his narrator reveals that the *Journal* was intended to be "antimythic," a representation of the now and here of London in 1665, with only a rhetorical bow to Defoe's 1722 audience.[22]

Here is a narrative that exactly fits Rader's model of a false true story. The significance of the *Journal* is not just that it claims that the *events* it chronicles happened—the same is true of such modern works as *In Cold Blood*—but that this memorial account is itself what it purports to be. Since Defoe and not H.F. is known to be its author, a bit of a problem remains that will have to be dealt with later. Unlike Moll, Crusoe, Jack, and Roxana, H.F. was created as a device of confirmation. The reader is not supposed to know that H.F. is a device, since the illusion of his natural reality was intended to be opaque. One may treat him as a novelistic character, or even as one would treat Moll, but this can be done only because even highly determined structures permit, as inadvertent consequences, other uses to be made of their elements. The *Journal* differs from the *Memoirs* and *Carleton* only because Defoe finally found a promising subject and invented a narrator absolutely appropriate to it.

Once more, the question seems to pivot on the nature of a narrator. Once again there is little consensus. Is H.F. only a more developed device than the Cavalier or does he interact with the other elements of story as Moll does? James Sutherland and, more recently, Louis Landa argue that it is Defoe's subject, the plague, which imposes a "certain order." Landa contends that H.F. "is not simply a utilitarian *persona*" but that nevertheless he "lacks the dimensions" of Crusoe, Moll, and the others. This view suggests a continuum of effect ranging from subject to character, rather than the more radical differences in use I see.[23] On the other hand is the thematic interpretation, pushing the book and H.F. ever closer to novelistic status. In this view, H.F. carries the same burden of communicating Defoe's beliefs that his other narrators do. The *Journal* becomes a vehicle for Defoe's ideological intention. Looking about him for a truth, Defoe finds one and follows neoclassical doctrine by fabulating a story to carry the didactic message. Even though H.F. specifically disavows "preaching a Sermon instead of writing a History" (p. 247), thematic ingenuity can dismiss the "vicarious experience" that would result and replace it with an ideological aim: the reader should learn from H.F. to embrace "an attitude compounded as the narrator's is of rationality and piety." It is not enough that H.F. serve as cicerone of the plague-year wonders; he must also guide the reader, as Ciceronian rhetorician, to moral truth. It is evident what happens when the uneven surface of pseudofactual narrative is asked to reflect an ideology back: interpretive variations fructify, no fecundity matching that of semantic analogy. What is to Starr exemplary, therefore, about H.F. is to Zimmerman "sinful presumption," an improper tempting of God's wrath by stubbornly remaining in the midst of death.[24] H.F.'s matter-of-fact reportorial role, once dismissed or overlooked, leads on easily to elevating aspects of his presence and function to the status of controlling idea. One must not ask how these

messages, indeed based on verifiable rhetorical "places" of the age—
like the need to combine rationality with piety—could ever have
endeared this book and many of Defoe's others to readers long after
Defoe's century was over. Such a question smacks not only of an
enfeebled historical consciousness, but also a naive distrust of histor-
icism: the widely believed notion that human thought and action are
best understood as the necessary products of an age. The implicit
syllogism runs thus: since they always write in order to communicate
their beliefs, and since their beliefs always reflect the historical
"moment," writers always express in whatever they write the ideas of
their time, no matter how commonplace they may be.

Asperity aside, this is all to say that if the existence of ideas in the
Journal cannot be disputed, their use and importance can. Even apart
from that complicated formal and evaluative question, one would
certainly be entitled to pass judgment on the profundity of Defoe's
thoughts as opposed, say, to the profundity of the experience in
which they are represented. As loosely as the *Journal* seems put
together, it makes a virtue of a great variety of elements, including
abstract ideas, in order to represent the moving and significant
experience itself. Except for brief and relatively inert passages in
which H.F., like the Cavalier, serves to grind some axe clearly
Defoe's, H.F.'s role is primarily that of a device of disclosure and
rhetorical control. If he is more interesting than the Cavalier, it is
only because the horrors he unveils require a more vitally involved
spokesman than do the military exploits of the stolid warrior. Yet,
because the direction of subordination remains from personality to
events and because the source of significance is the very historicity of
the 1665 plague, one can generalize complex personality from H.F.'s
role only at the risk of creating what is not there.

For instance, H.F.'s personal conflict about whether to flee or trust
in God, so replete with meaning for so many interpreters, finally
shuts off meaning because it has a nonsemantic function. In order for
the reader to accept the implausibility of a sensible man's remaining
amidst such horrors, Defoe must represent the process of thought

that led to the decision. He must even portray the internal deliberations as if they were most ordinary, thereby camouflaging what is objectively an unusual eccentricity on H.F.'s part. If the reasons H.F. gives for trusting to the "Direction . . . of Divine Power" (p. 10) seemed at all idiosyncratic or perverse, then Defoe risked calling attention to his solution of a problem of credibility.

Attempts to make H.F.'s deliberations novelistically or didactically purposeful therefore require the text to reward a cognitive operation that it is fashioned to preclude. Of course, texts in their infinite flexibility will accommodate almost any semantic analogy; but this text, to be understood, requires that one resist the exfoliation of analogy. The following passage, for example, so often analyzed, leads to interpretive dead ends if it must be endowed with more meaning than its function demands. In it, H.F. justifies spending so much time on the personal matter of why he stayed in London: "I have set this particular down so fully, because I know not but it may be of Moment to those who come after me, if they come to be brought to the same Distress, and to the same Manner of making their Choice and therefore I desire this Account may pass with them, rather for a Direction to themselves to act by, than a History of my actings, seeing it may not be of one Farthing value to them to note what became of me" (p. 8). Starr interprets this passage as evidence of Defoe's endorsement not only of "H.F.'s ultimate decision to stay in London" but also of the narrator's "mode of deliberating." Yet for Zimmerman, H.F. here reveals the opposite, a sinful presumption he will finally have to repent.[25] Neither reading does justice to either the passage's literal function in the text or to its complex disjunctiveness. Yet both Starr and Zimmerman reveal that they conceive of narrative meaning in the same abstract, extractive way. Within the illusion of historicity, H.F. simply explains the extended treatment of his own "History" in a journal whose ostensible subject is the history of a plague.

However, viewed with the external knowledge that H.F. is Defoe's creation, the passage is a storytelling device designed to preclude certain judgments. Apart from the demands of the sequence, Defoe may actually intend H.F. to be useful to readers who may someday face another plague (one was raging in Marseilles in 1720). Yet his use would still be as a reporter of what happened, and hardly as an example of what to do, as he himself recognizes when he later argues that the best course is to run away from such an infection. H.F.'s very reportorial function, in that it demands activities not only dangerous but to an extent foolhardy, disqualifies him as a model for imitation. A "mode of reasoning" that ends in a faulty conclusion hardly results in being endorsed, no matter how closely the process of justification may approach what Defoe elsewhere recommends. Nor is H.F.'s conduct assimilable to even the weakest pattern of spiritual autobiography, except by means of highly selective reading. With sufficient contentiousness, one could remark that a decision made on page 8, dismissed on page 14 ("I had no more Debate . . . on that Subject"), and referred to in passing only once more (p. 76), hardly establishes a pattern of repentance. Of more consequence, attempts to find complexity in H.F.'s conduct rather than in the subject he narrates can lead to outright misreading. Zimmerman, for example, argues that H.F. repents his decision to stay because he realizes he has sinned by presuming too much. What H.F. actually says is that he regrets staying in town because of the horrors he has witnessed: "I cannot say, but that now I began to faint in my Resolutions, my Heart fail'd me very much, and sorely I repented of my Rashness: When I had been out, and met with such terrible Things as these I have talked of; I say, I repented my Rashness in venturing to abide in Town" (p. 76). The only ambiguity is in H.F.'s employing the word "repent." Clearly, H.F. means that he *regrets* his decision, not because he believes he has offended God but because he has disregarded common sense—for which he has paid the price of witnessing soul-wrenching woe.

Given the demands of the illusion, perfectly cogent reasons, if not interpretively exciting ones, exist for H.F.'s vacillation and final decision to stay, as well as for his regretting that decision. The special horror of the plague emerges only if someone not only reports its devastations but explains and judges them. H.F. therefore needs to project a reliability that would doom a Moll or Roxana to flatness. The inexplicability of death stalking a city and not eccentric personality is the subject here, and H.F.'s cautious reluctance to proffer ultimate answers creates both confidence in him and wonder at the events. Yet his circumspection, the plausible attribute of a middle-aged businessman, clashes with his decision to remain in town. Only an arrant fool would venture among the pestiferous if he could escape, as H.F.'s brother tells him. The narrator's "mode of deliberating" matters only if we single it out—and a quantitatively minor element in a big book it is—and give it undue prominence. Defoe's handling of the problem of plausibility is so skillful that the contradiction seems no more than common human anomaly.

Yet a standard of appropriateness does convert this fairly mechanical matter of H.F.'s remaining into an integral and contributing element. Many possible reasons for H.F.'s actions were available, including the financial and familial ones his brother argues are not sufficient. The high seriousness of the decision and the plague context in which it occurs dictate that H.F.'s reasons not be frivolous. Attendance at Armageddon cannot depend on a few bales of dry goods. The situation requires religious deliberation, although, because H.F.'s remaining in London involves a special kind of passivity, we could not be sure Defoe himself would endorse H.F.'s decision. Again, the exigencies of factual replication require caution where authorial belief is involved. It would be absurd to dismiss either H.F.'s or Defoe's beliefs as unimportant; but it is equally absurd to assume that they are directly and unambiguously communicated in a work that is based on a kind of delusion. It is finally probable, although by no means sure, that Defoe, himself a sensible man, would concur with H.F.'s later recommendation: *the best Physick against the Plague is to run away from it*" (pp. 197–198).

I have spent so much time on this episode and the exegetic difficulties it has spawned because it is representative of a tendency in modern criticism of the *Journal* to generalize the specific experience of the Plague Year out of existence. The result is to overlook H.F.'s status as one of the least novelistic figures in English "fiction." He is not, of course, the wooden chronicler the Cavalier is, but that is only because he must convey much more of the collective human experience than the soldier did—although one could argue that the *Memoirs* would have been better if the Cavalier had, within the factual illusion, given us more of the common concerns of an army. Unlike the Cavalier, whose traits are dictated by the military subject, H.F.'s personality results as an amalgam of ordinary humanity, an imitation of plausible conduct and feeling amidst methodical horror. We do not give "one Farthing" what becomes of him, not because he lacks attraction, but because concern for him would deflect our attention away from London's agony. Defoe has therefore rightly prevented such concern. If one considers how easily he could have centered the entire story on the narrator's private fate, one can see how carefully Defoe has avoided personalizing him. Even when H.F. fears for his own safety, when he contracts a fever, or risks giving money to the pitiful boatman and his starving family, his fears and the reader's are for the collective fate of a populace. Moll fears for her life, and the reader fears for Moll.

H.F.'s role, then, is primarily that of a watcher. For this reason Defoe makes him an upright and relatively prominent citizen, one who would indeed be asked to be an "officer." By the same token, Defoe gives him his insatiable curiosity. Yet, as intrusive as he is, as interested in the lives of others as any of Henry James's narrators, one must follow his balanced and judicious report with superior inferential capacity indeed to feel "increasingly aware of his presence as he describes the course of the plague."[26] Even at his most vivid he seldom interacts with the flow of events, as Moll and Roxana habitually do. Nor are his sayings and doings informed by any principle of "surprise," as opposed to the wonders he sees; he draws no charmingly inapt "inferences." H.F. merely thinks and acts, one might say reacts, as one can recognize one probably would in a similar situation.

He walks into a tavern and discovers "hellish abominable Raillery," directed even at him, at a time when everyone should be on his knees (p. 65). His astonishment at such blasphemy is the reader's as well. He is "fill'd" with "Horror" and goes away "griev'd." Yet even after he reports that they all "died in a most deplorable Manner" (p. 66), he does not rush to point the obvious moral, as a very different narrator usually does in the *Due Preparations for the Plague*. Rather, H.F. dwells on their "Atheistical profane Mirth," as if he cannot accept it as a human possibility (p. 67). To argue that H.F.'s "self-assurance is shaken" by this episode is to reverse the clear subordination of his personality to his role as reporter of the absurd, grotesque, and anomalous in human conduct. Unlike James's watchers, who often approach voyeurism, it is not H.F.'s consciousness that is under scrutiny, but the wondrous and sometimes pitiful attempts of weak and sinful mortals to postpone or defy death. At such moments as the tavern scene, a judgment that centers on H.F.'s "self-assurance" would diminish the real significance of what the reader is seeing along with H.F.[27] As with Hemingway's Nick, knowing that Ole Andreson passively awaits death back in the rooming house, "It's too damned awful" to contemplate. Even H.F.'s ability to generate homilies is thwarted. He conjectures that surely "God would not think fit to spare . . . such open declared Enemies" (p. 68), but turns from judgment and condemnation back to exemplification again: more "Horror." H.F.'s reactions, as part of Defoe's rhetoric of factual treatment, not only enrich the verisimilar experience, they consistently turn our eyes outward, away from the concerns of the reporter himself and toward the puzzling-enough reality of the plague. No wonder, then, that Watson Nicholson naively thought the book "true."

What selfhood H.F. displays serves to help "represent those Times exactly to those that did not see them, and give the Reader due Ideas"—that is, accurate images—"of the Horror that every where presented it self" (p. 16). Defoe, one often hears, has little pictorial ability, much less a desire to appeal to the senses. It is not only in

Robinson Crusoe that, as Virginia Woolf noted, "Nature must furl her splendid purples."[28] The Cavalier, whose subject one might expect to call forth effective description, usually plods along with catchall generality: "This Calamity sure was the dreadfullest Sight that ever I saw; the Rage of the *Imperial* Soldiers was most intolerable, and not to be expressed; of 25000, some said 30000 People, there was not a Soul to be seen alive" (p. 44). Human suffering for the Cavalier is a fact to be tabulated with the other recurrent events of war. But this is not some Continental battleground, this is safe and sane London, the center of rational prosperity. How could this kind of daily horror take place here? Ten years before the *Journal*, Joseph Addison had pointed out the "pleasing Astonishment" resulting from an encounter with "any thing that is too big" for our "Capacity." If then the "Great" is supplemented by the "Uncommon," the pleasure of novelty, the mind luxuriates in a "double Entertainment," since the unusual can even bestow "Charms on a Monster."[29] It is H.F.'s function to try to convey something of the magnitude of London's suffering and the way in which the plague has put an end to all of the city's usual activities. The London plague therefore calls forth some of Defoe's most vivid description at the same time that H.F.'s attempts to "describe the Objects that appear'd" before him "every Day" are doomed to insufficiency by the nature of the task. It is not so much that "mere words" fail H.F. as it is that narrative itself cannot duplicate the historical power of the events.

> . . . after I have told you . . . that One Man being tyed in his Bed, and finding no other Way to deliver himself, set the Bed on fire with his Candle, which unhappily stood within his reach, and Burnt himself in his Bed. And how another, by the insufferable Torment he bore, daunced and sung naked in the Streets, not knowing one Extasie from another, I say, after I have mention'd these Things, What can be added more? What can be said to represent the Misery of these Times, more lively to the Reader, or to give him a more perfect Idea of a complicated Distress? [pp. 176–177]

Even a personal version of history falls short of the event's own profundity. H.F. reports the sounds of suffering, and they only add to the paradox of incommunicability: "Heaps and Throngs of People"—a nicely expressive redundancy—"would burst out . . . making a dreadful Clamour, mixt or Compounded of Skreetches, Cryings and Calling one another" (pp. 177–178). The fire that would engulf London the next year was at least visible, something to be resisted by the rational actions of those in its path. The unseen pestilence is something else. As in Sophocles' Thebes, "taking of thought is no spear for the driving away of the plague."[30] The force of the *Journal* depends on explanations of the inexplicable, rhetoric and inquiry alike doomed at utterance: "we could not conceive what to make of it . . . the Plague rag'd . . . beyond all I have express'd" (p. 178). At such moments, the affective heart of the *Journal*, H.F. turns from vain attempts, which are not, of course, vain at all, to describe the vagaries of sudden death to interpretation and conjecture, as if words, futile metonymy for the horror of the experience, can at least freeze it for an instant. He inclines originally to the view of comets as "Forerunners and Warnings" of divine wrath, but also cautions that astronomers assign "natural causes" for them (p. 20). The question, like that of why the innocent and holy perish alongside the corrupt and blasphemous, is insoluble. All H.F. can do is to show how such mysteries affected the "common People." He does so in a way that emphasizes the fruitlessness of trying to account for the plague: "But let my Thoughts, and the Thoughts of the Philosophers be, or have been what they will, these Things had a more than ordinary Influence upon the Minds of the common People, and they had almost universal melancholly Apprehensions of some dreadful Calamity and Judgment coming upon the City" (p. 20). The "thoughts" of the chronicler, or even of the professional logicians, do not matter next to the brooding or frenzied fears of those in mortal danger. When discussing amulets and charms, or the return of religious intolerance, H.F. refuses to "enter into Arguments" on "either or both Sides," instead presenting the issues "historically" (p. 176). He details not the theoretical arguments about the efficacy of charms but the consequences of trusting in them: those who did were "afterwards carried away in the Dead-Carts" (p. 33). What signify, he suggests, disputes among "Parties and Perswasions" when "on the other Side the Grave we shall be all Brethren again" (p. 176)?

H.F. always returns to the central, obdurate fact of the plague, its misery and death. Defoe knew, as did Samuel Johnson, that "All joy or sorrow for the happiness or calamities of others is produced by an act of the imagination." As remote from present experience as a plague might be, H.F.'s descriptions place the reader "for a time, in the condition of him whose fortune we contemplate."[31] H.F. asks, "What could make deeper Impressions on the Soul, than to see a Man almost Naked and got out of his House . . . come out of *Harrow-Alley* . . . run Dancing and Singing, and making a thousand antick Gestures, with five or six Women and Children running after him, crying, and calling upon him, for the Lord's sake to come back" (p. 171). Such passages are taken for granted by most interpreters of the *Journal*; but they, far more than the narrator's judicious commentary, contain the essence of the account. To argue that this representation of human suffering, all the more powerful because of the illusion that it is not represented but reported, is really subsidiary to some ideological message about reason, spiritual growth, or the urban experience is an indication that some modern criticism has gone too far in pursuit of what amount to abstract cultural clichés, at the expense of vitiating the force of the narrated experience. One should avoid inviting some future analysis of the "dehumanization of criticism." Even H.F.'s discussions of causes and policies, from which many critics derive the book's meaning, are finally subordinate to the scenes of suffering. It is as if H.F. turns his back on what he can neither explain nor really face up to in order to engage in the more comfortable activity of theorizing. In his response, and in his grim fascination with death and its environs, he is a paradigm of the reader's inability to imagine fully what London went through. It often "pierc'd" his "very Soul to hear the Groans and Crys of those who were thus tormented," yet he refuses to dwell on his own feelings. The sights, though permanently fixed in his memory, are best not recollected too vividly or too often.

The *Journal* could have progressed without H.F.'s presence being represented so fully; the illusion of historicity might then have been even more impenetrable. Yet, by showing H.F. simultaneously repelled by the horror of the plague and desiring desperately to understand it, Defoe lends factual reconstruction a rhetorical and affective power the *Memoirs* lacked. Starr argues that H.F. is concerned as much "with interpreting the plague as with graphically recreating it."[32] On the contrary, except for the spread of the plague, which H.F. explains with the contagion theory, he serves less to mediate than to present questions, like any veritable historian. Yet his uncertainty functions rhetorically also. He can no more decide why the disease descended than he can convey its full horror. His puzzlement, which Defoe means to be construed as no more than the natural response of an ordinary man, bears close scrutiny. The plague, like the workings of God, is a mystery shrouded in darkness, like the interiors of houses shut up by public order. "It is true," H.F. remembers, that "Masters . . . were bound by the Order" to report their families had sickened. Yet many "think themselves Sound" when they are not. H.F. next gives an example of the collective fate of such unfortunates: they "walk'd the Streets till they fell down Dead." Then follow particular details enabling the reader to identify with a single situation: "not that they were suddenly struck with the Distemper, as with a Bullet . . . but that they really had the Infection in their Blood long before, only, that, as it prey'd secretly on the Vitals, it appear'd not till it seiz'd the Heart with a mortal Power, and the Patient died in a Moment, as with a sudden Fainting, or an Apoplectick Fit" (pp. 167–168). Successively more specific situations, until it is time to start the cycle over again, would seem to lead to greater understanding. What usually happens instead is that the plague ends up overwhelming any attempt to make sense of it or to decide how to deal with it. H.F., himself involved as an official "Examiner," has his own opinion of the practice of quarantining entire households. Not only was it a severe injustice to those still healthy, the policy "did not answer the End" (p. 170). Here at last, it seems, is some certainty. But immediately it vanishes: "after the Funerals became so many . . . all the Remedies of that Kind had been used till they were found fruitless" (pp. 170–171). General propositions lead downward to human suffering; comforting explanations disappear as the plague's untouchable and unknowable force moves on.

I do not mean to imply, as does Frank Kermode in his recent book, *The Genesis of Secrecy*, that it is an inherent property of narrative to reflect the inscrutability of all experience.[33] The search for some universal quality of narrative, fascinating as it is when the pursuit is carried out by someone of Kermode's ability, leads away from Defoe's accomplishment. Defoe wrote many works of history and biography before he discovered Crusoe and the full possibilities for feigning. Many of these earlier works, like the *Memoirs of . . . Shrewsbury*, served the ends of faction. Some might mistake them for truth, but those on the "inside" knew they were required to extract a meaning hidden under the reportorial surface. The *Journal*, on the contrary, achieves it significance by scrupulously avoiding the usual strategies of novelistic, allegorical, or parabolic meaning. London does not stand for anything. It is not a sign but a self-referring state of existence, a real city vibrating to its own fevered heartbeat. If one is fond of interpretive paradoxes, one may call London the central "character" in the *Journal*. But to do so suggests an allusive potentiality denied both by Defoe's use of literal verisimilitude and by the mystery of the plague itself. One may compare Defoe's London to Camus's Oran, but the comparison, on anything but the most general and analogical grounds, only succeeds in pointing up the radical separation of the two narrative worlds, the historical and the latent. In Camus's parable, the setting, the disease, the being and actions of the characters, all intentionally signify in ways foreign to the *Journal*. If it should be learned tomorrow that Oran had never been visited by a plague, that should not change the way *The Plague* is read. If one learned that London was not beset in 1665, the *Journal* would lose an indeterminate but probably substantial amount of its historical power. Camus's story creates its own world of meaning. Defoe's depends on what happened in 1665.[34]

I suggested in the first chapter that Defoe's serious attempts to lie like the truth ended with the *Journal*. In fact, after wrestling with the novelistic problems *Roxana* presented him, he turned to criminal lives and feigned memoirs, such as those of Jonathan Wild and George Carleton, that differ from his earlier and greater works in that they do not utilize much of a sense of personage. These works are primarily sensationalist or journalistic and do not take him beyond what he had achieved. Certainly he never found another subject for factual reconstruction as richly evocative as the Plague Year, nor one that made such excessive demands on invention and rhetoric for the sake of a generically historical effect.

The *Journal* is also the last well-known example of invented history, although feignings and impersonations are found in later travel literature, pulp fiction of the American West, and even in pornographic narrative. As a viable tradition, whether subliterary or not, pseudohistory disappears. The spectacular success of *Pamela*, indeed, the establishment of the novel as a popular and lucrative, if not an immediately reputable, genre eliminated one reason for lying like the truth. As William Nelson remarks, no matter how much "editing" an earlier pseudohistorian practiced, he could not "at the same time claim credit for inventing his matter," and "such self-denial is not characteristic of imaginative authors."[35] Whatever social and economic influences bore on the rise of middle-class realism, the creation of viable forms to employ that realism also depended on developments in aesthetics and criticism, as when Fielding finally persuades Richardson that the pose of being only the editor of letters he has invented not only is no longer necessary but a bit silly. Other influences were surely at work, although this is not the place system-atically to explore them. Invented "eyewitness" accounts risked exposure once newspapers became popular. Feigned history declined also in part because professional historians and biographers such as Gibbon and Johnson took over the field. Invented memoirs disappeared as the rise of literacy transformed the populace into a bank of potential private and public chroniclers of self.

Whatever the English novel was to become, its overt fictionality and patterned fabulousness was a possibility unknown, except in dramatic guises, to the author of the *Journal*. H.F. is a product of an author who celebrates the fruits of memory, who knows, as did Aristotle, that humans naturally wish to drink deeply from the well of pain and ecstasy that is the past, to know about and in a sense experience moments forever lost, just because they really did happen. Such has always been the attraction of history. The novel, in its traditional forms, satisfies different yearnings: causality, completeness and closure, the illusion, at least, that in *this* tightly made world, if not in the wider one, events are understandable. These comfortable and comforting assumptions that the traditional novel implies were soon challenged. The "want of discretion" Henry James decried in Trollope, the opprobrious concession that "the events he narrates have not really happened, and that he can give his narrative any turn the reader may like best" implies "that the novelist is less occupied in looking for the truth . . . than the historian."[36] Novelists since James have imbibed an even deeper skepticism than this one, however, a distrust of absolutes, even of determinate or objective knowledge itself. Outside of the scientist's laboratory, all is chaos. Since one can know nothing about values, except their relativity, authors must not presume to guide. They must be content to show.[37] And what is the point of fabulating if not to suggest a moral order of some sort? So it is that the spirit of the *Journal* rises as one competitor to fill the void left when some, if not all, novelists lose faith in their craft, one that depended for two hundred years on conveying structured values in structured fiction. Is it not better, now that fabulating, when it is risked, avoids the guidance of strong pattern and manipulation of the reader—both evidence of naiveté—to reconstruct actual events, to "represent" the psyches and traumas of "characters," like Nat Turner, who the reader knows actually lived out their sordid existences? Two hundred years after a distrust of fiction making gave rise to the *Memoirs of a Cavalier* and *A Journal of the Plague Year*, a very different agnosticism moves Mailer, Capote, and many others to compose nonfiction. They do so artfully, of course. Yet the sense of "this really happened" pervades these works as surely as it does some of Defoe's.

IV

The Captain and Moll

THE WORLD OF DISCOURSE was once considered a safer place than it is today. When Samuel Johnson set out to define the principles of definition, he assumed at least a psychological, if not ideal, reality to which words corresponded: "for as nothing can be proved but by supposing something intuitively known, and evident without proof, so nothing can be defined but by the use of words too plain to admit a definition." Words had a solidity no less than that of Johnson's rock, which he kicked to "refute" Berkeley's theory of immateriality. Today, such notions seem naive. In his discussion of Benjamin Constant, Todorov confirms Constant's opposition to the idea that "signs can be faithful to their designata. To suppose that words can faithfully account for things is to admit that (1) 'things' are there, (2) words are transparent, harmless, without consequence for what they designate, (3) words and things enter into a static relation. But none of these implicit propositions is true, according to Constant."[1]

The more radical purveyors of this view would have it, therefore, that we have indulged ourselves in a sort of wish fulfillment, a hedonistic orgy of meaning-seeking that finally was, at worst, solipsistic, or at best, reductive. This is a much more fundamental question than the one involved in my earlier observation that some critics seem to have created meaning which Defoe's texts do not enforce. The debate can be followed on the pages of *New Literary History* and *Critical Inquiry*. For my purposes, it will have to suffice to suggest that even if all narrative were finally treacherous and unreliable—obviously, I do not think it is—historical and fictional narrative would not necessarily betray us in the same ways. Indeed, in one sense, a chasm stretches between the two realms. Veritable history, or what is taken to be true, refers, or at least pretends to, and in its pretending is an important part of how it affects us. The relationship between an event and a narrative of what happened is analogous to that between signified and signifier. Even if it is true that to "designate . . . to verbalize . . . is to change" whatever one names,[2] one is still left, within the text, with an illusion of referentiality that somehow demands its integrity, paradoxically, even if one knows by external information that the referentiality is, as in Defoe, delusive. The *Journal* makes precisely such strong claims. It asks that one "overlook" for a time the knowledge that the story is a fabrication. It is among the paradoxes of literary experience that one can go on construing H.F.'s words as if they actually referred. The *Journal*, and all such successful "lies," like Madame D'Aulnoy's *Travels into Spain*, which fooled so many for so long, in part because readers wanted to be fooled, therefore satisfy Jacques Barzun's four criteria "by which history may be known . . . Narrative, Chronology, Concreteness, and Memorability." One need make only a slight, but important, modification of his final standard: the " 'story' is, of course, intended as truth," must be emended to, "intended to be taken as truth." The *Journal* will not accommodate its being read successfully as a coherent novel, in part because the "upshot of any . . . part is not a simple formulated truth, but the communication of many truths, in an artful mixture of order and disorder addressed not to the geometric but to the intuitive mind."[3] By a curious strategy, Defoe has overcome the "law, according to which a speech becomes false if it tries to be true." At least, the *Journal*'s power resides in that attempt.[4] The intention of the author would seem to deny and overturn the intention of the work, but it cannot do so. The latter remains historical. This curious chiasmus of covert and avowed intentions makes crucial the decision of *how* to talk about the *Journal*.

If the *Journal* is considered as imitated history of the personal kind, most of the formal and affective problems clear up. Yet the solution is not so simple with Defoe's other works, as was seen with the mélange that is *Robinson Crusoe*. *Moll Flanders*, culminating a series of transformations and refinements of possibilities Defoe uncovered in *Robinson Crusoe*, is an exception by virtue of its unity. *Captain Singleton* is at a middle stage in the process of development and transformation and proceeds on no single impulse. *Colonel Jack* leads away from the celebration of personality and impinges on the territory of the novel, finally realized only in *Roxana*; even so, Defoe repeatedly backs away from Jack's possibilities as a novelistic character. With the exception of *Moll Flanders*, all these works fluctuate among principles of being and therefore refuse to teach, in any coherent fashion, how they are to be read. Events, personality, moral and social polemic, all alternate as successive foci, precluding orientation within the text.

For awhile, then, I shall be forced to examine a number of fragmented tendencies in Defoe, at least until it is time to discuss *Moll Flanders* and the conclusion of *Roxana*. For now, the question involves the set of modifications necessary for Defoe to transform the mixed mode of *Robinson Crusoe* into the relative homogeneity of *Moll Flanders*, a series that leads through *Captain Singleton* (1720). In this line of development, Defoe works toward a special kind of fictive unity, but one that culminates in a dead end because it results in *Moll Flanders*. This formulation may seem perverse, although I shall try to show that it helps explain Moll's enduring attraction and the difficulties critics have had with her book. Finally, I shall note briefly the same tendency toward nonnovelistic fictionality in *Colonel Jack* while at the same time remarking its unrealized, or aborted, novelistic potentialities.

Disposable Personality: Captain Bob

Defoe begins *The Life, Adventures, and Pyracies, of the Famous Captain Singleton* as if he intends to exploit the attractions of vivid personality discovered the year before in *Robinson Crusoe*. "Capt. Bob" has an ironic attitude toward his former self that assimilates him to Moll, Jack, and Crusoe. He would like very much to tell about his "Originals" and "Ancestors," but unfortunately he "can look but a very little way" into his "Pedigree."[5] After the success of *Robinson Crusoe*, it is not surprising that Defoe now seems intent on doing something to exploit the human interest inherent in situations of isolation. The opening of *Singleton*, therefore, seems to set in motion a kind of forlorn *Bildungsroman*, in which Bob will successively be stripped of all the traditional resources of identity. Violations of his humanity, like being sold for "Twelve Shillings of another Woman" (p. 2), will finally lead to estrangement and then crime. Immediately one sees something that is a prototype, although more clear cut, of Moll's ironic detachment, akin to her seeing her mother's thievery as "borrowing," in Bob's comment that his "good *Gypsey Mother* . . . happened in Process of Time to be hang'd . . . for some of her worthy Actions, *no doubt*" (p. 2). Not only is the "hero's" body denied a resting place as he shuffles about, his right to ordinary human relationships is canceled. Finally winding up with a "Master of Ship" whom he "pleased . . . so well," Bob becomes the master's **"own Boy."** Now follows the accretion of resonating details that gives Crusoe's island life so much personal density. Bob says that he "would have called" this captain "Father," but the master "would not allow it, for he had Children of his own" (p. 3). Looking back, Bob refuses to lament his isolation. Like Defoe's other outcasts and orphans, he stoically accepts the past, in part because he has managed to survive it: "It is in vain to reflect . . . who my Father and Mother were . . . it would make but a needless Digression to talk of it" (p. 2). Natural parents, surrogate fathers, human comfort itself, all the ordinary underpinnings of normal identity were long ago swept away. To imagine such a past, to create through one's fancy a childhood that did not exist, becomes a vain exercise in storytelling. Stories invite digressions, but the "Life" must stick to what happened.

With the material of memory unattractive at best, the young Bob dismisses the future as well. The "Disaster" of being taken by an "Algerine" pirate rover he "was not much concerned at," even when his kind master was wounded and "very barbarously used," frequently a euphemism in Defoe for the utmost excruciation. He becomes "concerned"—a curiously bloodless and distant term, a kind of index of dissociation—only when the pirates beat him "most unmercifully with a flat Stick on the Soles" of his feet (p. 3). He is, again, "not much concerned" at his "Captivity," from which he is shortly delivered by a Portuguese man-of-war, only to find himself in Lisbon, friendless and now without the resources of language to make his wants understood.

This situation is ideal for the portrayal of interactive personality, in which direction Defoe seemed steadily to gravitate unless he concentrated on a strict factual illusion. Critics invariably focus on these vivid opening scenes, passages in which a strong sense of the depth of Bob's alienation is portrayed effectively. Indeed, while Crusoe laments the "sin" that separated him physically from the company of others, Bob's self-portrait reveals a boy who suffers from what a modern sociologist would call "anomie." The retrospective narrator, at this point in the story, is quite a different case. He has lived to command men, acquire both a fortune and an adopted brother, in the Quaker William, wed a wife in William's sister, and ease his troubled conscience by repenting. He is able to look back on his younger self with irony. That double vision actually seems to function at the start of the book. The discrepancy between the now-respectable narrator and the younger man, who cared for little but deviltry, is marked: "I was diligent indeed, but I was very far from honest; however, they thought me honest, which by the Way, was their very great Mistake" (p. 5). The narrator supplies reasons, in his experience and personality, for his own nature: "Education" he had "none"; he was "either so young, or so stupid" that he had "escaped the Grief and Anxiety"—normal feelings, that is—usually attendant on "Dangers and desperate Circumstances" (p. 5), having no sense of "their Tendency and Consequences" (p. 11).

In these first few pages one learns more about Bob than about any of Defoe's other narrators until Moll. Even the opening of *Robinson Crusoe* does not match the particularity of Bob's account, in part because Crusoe's personality is expressed in sets of oppositions and tensions, such as duty versus inclination, that have the ring of cliché. In a way, Bob is the initial testing ground for the sort of implicatory depth, really only an illusion of depth, which Defoe would achieve with Moll, Jack, and Roxana. It is not difficult to see how, with a different set of narrative strategies at his disposal, and an inclination to enact different episodic transformations than the merely additive, Defoe might have gone on to delineate a novelistic action centering on Bob's continuing struggle to assimilate himself to society and exorcise the effects of early neglect. Indeed, the voice of the narrator indicates that in the silence and empty space between the young Bob and himself is precisely such a story. The implied question underlying such a progressive sequence would have been how Bob got to be what he did as a *result* of his experiences and his reflections on them, a moral movement resembling Pip's. Short of such an accomplishment, which was beyond Defoe, he could have represented a continuing interaction of personality with a hostile, brutal pirate society. That Defoe chooses to tell neither of these stories only indicates that he is not yet fully aware of the potentialities inhering in personalities represented from the inside, or that he as yet does not know how to sustain a technique to that end. For whatever reasons, Defoe's beginning of *Singleton* turns out to be infertile. Bob becomes just another witness.

The neglect of such possibilities in Defoe is virtually paradigmatic and entails certain consequences. Whenever Defoe's attention shifts away from his narrator's psyche, either because he is more interested in the "what" than the "who" of experience, or because the ongoing significance is primarily communal, one can be almost certain the point of view will shift from the solitary "I" to the collective "we." The original example of this mutation is Crusoe, who speaks of the group almost any time he is not alone. Yet the practice is virtually an unvarying principle of Defoe's stories, part of their fabulational grammar, at least until Defoe discovers that it is harmful to the effect he aims for in *Moll Flanders*. Jack's usual reference matches his isolated existence, but it changes to the collective when the fate of his small, impoverished commonalty—he and his two "brothers" sleeping amidst thieves and murderers in the warm ashes of a glass-bottle factory—becomes for Defoe, even briefly, a more productive trope to investigate. Bob is no exception. He shifts into the plural so soon that the book's nature is immediately revealed. In 1720, Defoe still thinks of experience as primarily external. Even though the beginning of the story intimated that Defoe realized the potential depth inherent in a narrative double view, self reflecting on younger self, Bob's story quickly becomes a summary of what one might expect to hear from a competent, if unimaginative, travel writer who also happens to have been a pirate. Having begun with a situation and a persona that, for their promise to be realized, demanded continued probing of the consequences of ostracism, Defoe instead undermines the very basis of that premise.

The turning point occurs when Defoe drops Singleton off on Madagascar with the other mutineers, and allows him opportunity to distinguish himself and become a leader. This is a probable stage in the development of a boy who will become the self-confident man who narrates his own story; but here, Bob's mind and personality do not cause his development, it simply happens. The ensuing journey across Africa, fascinating as adventure and as geographical speculation, is at the same time an inappropriate scene for the representation of private musings. Yet, because Defoe's skill in handling complex interactions among characters, dramatic relationships, is still deficient, the communal point of view results in the same flat clichés of the *Memoirs*: "unpassable Desarts to go over, no Carriages, Camels or

Beasts . . . to carry our Baggage . . . wild and ravenous Beasts . . . Lions, Leopards, Tigers, Lizards, and Elephants . . . Nations of Savages . . . barbarous and brutish to the last Degree, Hunger and Thirst . . . in one Word, Terrors" (pp. 47–48). Would that one word might suffice. Instead, the reader is inundated with adventures designed to prove to the armchair excursionist what wonderful variety exists in the uncharted wild. Gone here is even the principle of confirmation De Quincey found in the *Memoirs*: "in all this, as there is nothing at all amusing, we conclude that . . . such particulars . . . were true." In all this, as there is nothing that at least was not intended to amuse, one therefore concludes that an "epitomizing" hand has taken over to give the narrator's "Harvest of *Wild Oats*" (p. 137).

Bob's personality resurfaces for a few brief moments. Sometimes, given the requirements of the action, he simply disagrees with his companions: "I had more Mind all the while . . . to have gone Northward . . . but for the present I held my Tongue" (p. 109). The absence of any portrayed psychological conflict is reminiscent of the early Crusoe, and here the absence contrasts sharply with the vivid opening of Singleton's story. At times Bob takes on a certain amount of vividness only to call to mind how dangerous the group's ventures were: "I consented to every thing . . . however hazardous . . . however improbable the Success" (p. 44). Intermittent reminders that this is adventure experienced by the narrator form part of the rhetoric of factual replication—although of course the reader is not to respond to it as such. Bob assumes command because he finds the Portuguese "void of Counsel" and "Presence of Mind," needing someone to "go before, and encourage them by Example" (pp. 54–55). Bob points up that his march across Africa was the "most desperate and impracticable Attempt that ever Men went about in the World" (p. 55). Perhaps there is always a need in factual replication for such claims, since the text offers events that have as their justification for being reported the inherent interest of their having occurred. (*Field and Stream* authors decline chronicling expeditions on which they see nary a trout.) Bob also serves to impart a sense of progression to what, in terms of actual development toward anything or even revelation of personality, is really a static sequence. There exists a residual effect, however, of his having been portrayed so vividly in the beginning. At any time he "enters" the story again, he will seem more important, within the factual illusion, than he objectively is. Not until the end of the book, when he and his "brother," William, decide that, having plundered at will for years, it may now be time to repent, does Bob reacquire some of the vitality he had at the beginning. This, too, is in part illusory, since Bob's presence now is a function of his interaction with the Quaker, who is represented as more complex even than the narrator. Their friendship, although it is only an additive operation of pairing, heralds the interdependence of Roxana and Amy.

Singleton is not, then, an innovation in any important sense. Like parts of *Robinson Crusoe*, it proceeds by adding together elements from the general paradigm, wondrous events. The relationship, at least in the beginning, between experiencing self and retrospective chronicler has been complicated to a certain extent, although the strategy does not seem to have caught Defoe's imagination. He prefers to go on piling wonder on top of wonder, clearly if inexplicably believing that the syntax of Crusoe's story before and after the island episodes really maps out the way to narrative success. The genuine innovation of *Singleton* remains in its undeveloped possibilities. Once Defoe discovers that the dual vision, complicated even further, can coexist with the liveliest sense of events experienced and not just described, he will be on his way to *Moll Flanders*. Once he discovers that the retrospective view presents opportunities for demarking entire sequences of events and creating within the narrow circle *causal* operations, he will be on to the basis of *Roxana*, and indeed of the traditional novel itself. *Singleton* remains a showcase for situations linked by the most mechanical of means, even when signs of Bob's growth of maturity or understanding glimmer momentarily to approach a step closer to the conclusion—always defined, until

Roxana, as the arbitrary point at which storytelling can end because the storyteller's present time has been reached. Unlike novelistically ordered experience, which requires the reader's acquiescences or denials, the event that is true, or pretends to be, turns both author and reader inward. Standards for generating significance can then only be produced from the resources of individual associations. Even the necessity for comment or interpretation becomes a matter of idiosyncratic judgment, so that some events the reader may feel call for generalization Defoe may leave naked on the page.

And when Defoe does comment, meaning arises not from a process of imagining what Bob might plausibly believe, except for early in the story, but from Defoe's own convictions. In the reportorial mode, belief is often inserted, not elicited from a set of probabilities within the configurations of personality and event. Experience and interpretation are related by coordination: Singleton did . . . from which Singleton determined . . . On the other hand is the vividly personalized narrator, who very well may espouse beliefs Defoe does not share or about which he has no strong opinion. When functioning personality fades, as it does in *Singleton*, one can be fairly confident that ideological units have originated straight from Defoe's own set of convictions. There will always be some pressures on the narrative that will bend this general principle, as with the *Memoirs*. Economy and episodic motivation may dictate the inclusion of certain ideas. The violation of economy, as when Moll and Roxana discourse excessively on the unhappy plight of women in this sexist society, can signal, conversely, that Defoe has interrupted his own imaginative continuum in order to sermonize. In like manner, contradiction can indicate authorial belief in *Singleton*. For example, Bob has "learnt several material Things" in his voyage "among the *Portuguese*," among them "to be an errant Thief and a bad Sailor," since the Portuguese are "the best Masters for Teaching both these, of any Nation in the World" (p. 5). One might expect this "aside" would suffice, especially since Defoe must know that within a few pages Singleton will cast his lot with these same reprobates. Yet the narrator continues the diatribe against the Portuguese, a "Nation the most perfidious," he contends, "and the most debauch'd, the most insolent and cruel, of any that pretend to call themselves Christians," men for whom "Thieving, Lying, Swearing, Forswearing" and "abominable Lewdness" are the "stated Practice" (p. 6).

One searches in vain, however, if one seeks in the poetics of fabulation a principle of subordination for these beliefs. One might stretch a point and argue that Bob's stridency lends him a certain combative, appropriate reality; one may even expect, this early, that experience will change Bob's mind, that he will learn to think better of these men. Indeed, what is seen of his companions on their perilous trek across Africa contradicts Bob's prejudice. But there is no process of mind-changing, no real moral dimension to Bob's beliefs. One must conclude that authorial belief, out of all proportion in its vituperation, has taken over, just as it does when Gulliver rails against the Dutch. Gulliver, however, consistently functions as a communicative device for Swift, who schools us to his covert intentions. No such system of signification exists most of the time in Defoe. One may know that Defoe did not admire the Portuguese, but only by external corroboration and by the probabilities of how meaning *might* arise in pseudofactual texts. There is no positive coding going on.[6]

Captain Singleton returns the readers, therefore, to the several worlds of narrative coexisting uneasily between the covers of *Robinson Crusoe*. In its lucid but brief beginning sketch of a boy abandoned and alone, the book signals the possibilities for interpenetrating event and personality that would lead to *Moll Flanders*. Yet far more consistently Defoe deals here with the wonders and frantic movement characteristic of older narrative traditions, like the one that spawned *The Unfortunate Traveler*. Only the beginning and sections of the conclusion solicit the clarity of the pervasive "I," the unity of the solitary consciousness at work on the materials of perception and mind. Yet, at the same time he was contemplating the "historical" illusion that would result in the *Journal*, Defoe planned a book that would develop as an end the principal pleasures and meanings he had uncovered on Crusoe's island and at the beginning of *Singleton*. The intense and unremitting focus on the mental life of a narrator leads away from both the experiential particularity of pseudohistory and the subordination of moral specificity characteristic of the novel. Such a refinement of the possibilities of "false true stories" leads to *Moll Flanders*.

Moll Flanders: Inside and Out

Commencing *Moll Flanders* therefore placed Defoe at a crossroads. He wanted to maintain the posture that he was only presenting the memoirs of another, in part because storytelling was not yet quite respectable, in part because he believed readers derived more benefit from accounts they believed true. More technically, his expertise, one might even say his faith, rested with the individual episode. The Puritan view of experience might well provide his stories with a kind of retrospective unity; but in the vital stirrings of the subject's own experiences, unity is an optical illusion resulting from the myopia of ego. The retrospective memoir reflects this chaos of life's flow while projecting, artlike, a sense of order and causality, even though that sense frequently in Defoe is a chimera.

Moll's book, then, is like what Roland Barthes calls a "lover's discourse." "Throughout any love life," Barthes reflects, "figures occur to the lover without any order, for on each occasion they depend on an (internal or external) accident. Confronting each of these incidents (what 'befalls' him), the amorous subject draws on the reservoir (the thesaurus?) of figures, depending on the needs, the injunctions, or the pleasures of his image-repertoire." The material of Moll's story falls into separate categories. Episodes could be classified according to whether they involve relations with men, or theft, or any other highly general category. They form a set of paradigms, like grammatical categories, on which Defoe can draw in order to maintain his vaunted "Variety." Yet, as Barthes says of the lover's discourse, "No logic links the figures, determines their contiguity: the figures are non-syntagmatic, non-narrative; they are Erinyes; they stir, collide, subside, return, vanish with no more order than the flight of mosquitoes.'"[7] Just as the lover's musings are linked only by their presence in the mind of the same lover, and their sequential, though not patterned, existence, Moll's episodes appear, while we are trapped within them, to have the randomness of reported experience.

The analogy will finally break down, as will be seen. But for now, it is enough to show how this illusion of disjointedness has led to so many difficulties with the book. In her imperviousness to criticism, Moll seems much more like the opaque figure of a *nouveau roman* than she does the lucid and potentially understandable character of the traditional novel. Long after Moll, Robbe-Grillet was to object to the "heroes" of traditional fiction, the manipulated creations that, far more than Moll, came to dominate prose fiction. From Richardson and Fielding to Hardy and Conrad, characters had been "constantly solicited, caught up, destroyed" by their authors' value-charged rhetoric, "ceaselessly projected into an immaterial and unstable *elsewhere*, always more remote and blurred." They had been, for whatever purpose, employed by the creator, not allowed their own integrity.

Moll, like Robbe-Grillet's "future hero," remains "on the contrary, *there*," oblivious to one's wishes, even to one's "commentaries." Moll is not *disponible*, or, depending on how one wishes to create narrative meaning, she is infinitely so. In one sense, the reader must generate her meaning, since Defoe does not. In another sense, following Robbe-Grillet's argument, the reader cannot "fill" Moll's interpretive spaces because Defoe has tried to leave no fissures in Moll's presentation. Those he has left—contradictions, for example—are inadvertant, nonfunctioning. Interpretation of her, therefore, begins to "seem useless, superfluous," if not, as Robbe-Grillet says of his "heroes," "improper."[8] Defoe applies no such aesthetic, much less moral or ontological, absolute to Moll. Something else, reflected in the dust-devil swirl of conflicting theories about her, shuts off interpretation or renders it hopelessly indeterminate. In his

preoccupation with the integrity of the single, verisimilar episode—
Defoe's "thesaurus" of "figures"—he has replicated the local ambiguity of a real memoir. Moll, as ostensible memorialist, provides no
more of a referential "framework" within which she may be judged
than do Pepys or Boswell for themselves. The illusion of self-reference
precludes her being seen, within her episodes, as a means to some end
not contained within the circle of her own perceptions. She is a
narrative exemplification of Gödel's Proof: there is no way to confirm
or refute her being as long as the reader remains inside her system, her
text.

The overall form of *Moll Flanders* does not emerge as an object of
contemplation by the ordinary process of fitting part to part to derive
a whole. Parts, like Moll herself, have edges that cannot be rubbed
off. The entire story may have a meaning, but the significance of each
episode results, as it does in the reader's experience of his own life's
"episodes," from an act of individual will. The wiliest deconstruc-
tionist would strive to no avail—or perhaps to certain success—over
Moll's text, both because there is no strong system and because no
clear authorial intention emerges from episodes. One may step out of
the book, as I shall argue shortly, and perceive an intention to conceal
intention, which could then be deconstructed; but that is an infinite
circularity, always self-confirming. If the illusion succeeds, the question of the intention of Moll's story should not arise, at least not from
the diachronic flow of the episodes themselves. Moll comments on all
things as she sees fit, What does her story comment on? Like the new
novel, *Moll Flanders* attempts to affirm nothing, a nice paradox in
itself. The reasons are different for Defoe and for Robbe-Grillet, of
course. Assertion in the modern world is self-refutation. As Barthes
says, "Everything I do has a meaning (hence I can *live*, without
whining), but this meaning is an ineffable finality: it is merely the
meaning of my strength."[9] For many modern authors, assertion has
become a joke on the self as well as on the reader. So the author
withdraws for primarily ontological reasons, aesthetic ones following
in their trail. Yet no one doubts that it is a new *novel* for which

Robbe-Grillet and others have served as collaborative midwives. Defoe, on the other hand, distrusts not assertion per se, few writers having tendered more opinions on more subjects, but fiction that reveals by its patterned signification its own fictitiousness. He maintains the local inertia and silence of literal truth because to do otherwise would ensure that the overall fictional purpose became manifest page by page. He writes fiction he does not want to be experienced locally as fictional.

Yet Defoe's self-denial, or timidity, does not extend to the whole. It is doubtful, in fact, whether authors can, for whatever reason, withdraw far enough from their works to accomplish what Robbe-Grillet advocates, unless they are willing to pay a tremendous price. Even selection of what to represent implies choice, and choice implies value. Once it is understood that Moll's episodes have been selected according to a standard of refinement, one can see that the local illusion of factuality is itself illusory. The whole of *Moll Flanders* is judged to be a product of some intelligence other than Moll's without positive evidence of that presence being given within episodes. Two intentions are at work, and they do not "merge." *Moll Flanders* is a collection of episodes drawn from truthlike paradigms. Its syntax is clearly fictional. Many critics have felt this disjunctiveness without being able to explain it. It is implied in the common observation that Moll's odyssey could easily be lengthened, shortened, or rearranged, but that the book is nevertheless a novel. Defoe's old and well-learned reportorial skills must coexist with his growing desire to organize represented randomness into a whole that will reflect, if nothing more, the control of art. Episodic fragmentation, Crusoe's confused but mightily various ramblings, had brought credibility; the historicity of the *Journal* achieved an affective coherence. In *Moll Flanders*, Defoe sought ways to impose fictional form on materials that would still retain the superficial opacity of real events. As in most crossings of intention, the result is more difficult to analyze than the intersecting impulses. There is the liveliest sense of random variety in Moll's life. Yet one recognizes, after pulling back from the flow of story, just how carefully the illusion has been arranged. The product is a book that the reader experiences as a result of one semiotic system but can understand only by attending to another. As Walter Wilson said long ago, Moll's story is "an epitome," a compendium of the essential pleasures of autobiographical narrative, ones possible only intermittently in actual memoirs and diaries. Defoe makes his book a collection of such moments.

That such an unusual design does not approximate the later novel should be apparent. Defoe still refuses, as so many have argued, to judge Moll page by page, declining therefore to create *himself* as an internal, purposeful presence. Values and events do not fuse. At least the beliefs that give rise to this type of prose fiction do not, as they try to do in traditional novels, help in any discernible fashion to determine the local experience of the narrative. Defoe plays no omnipotent Intercessor, no Jehovah or Zeus, preferring instead the role of impersonal deity, presiding from afar. To meddle in his story contradicts all his old habits, as well as the underlying beliefs about storytelling with which he is either, as one chooses to see it, encumbered or blessed. Even so, once he has permitted some principle other than lying like the truth to enter in, he has at least taken a step toward creating his own presence in the story, even if, like Moll herself, it refuses to interpret its own existence.

With a few important exceptions that will be treated later, episodes in *Moll Flanders* retain all the conventional appurtenances of truth, as Rader has demonstrated. Cause and effect do not operate in any consistent fashion. Yet neither does one find the paradox of a consistent, causative principle of fortuity, as in *Tom Jones*. Seldom can the nature or quality of episodic closure be predicted, although there is indeed a principle of closure at work, to be examined later, because it is a part of the book's syntax but not present in any of the book's paradigmatic categories. The local premise of Moll's existence is that she acts as a natural person would act. These features of the book's individual episodes, and a few others, lead Rader to argue that the book makes full sense only if it is understood as a "simulated naive incoherent autobiography." Defoe intends to present "the incidents as if they were not invented but merely reported." Moll's aimless recitation, the lack of any "sense of full consistency either of psychological portraiture or implicit ethical judgment," her languid manner of relating sensational incidents—all indicate Defoe intended readers of *Moll Flanders* and his other first-person narratives to "construe" the "matter as real."[10]

In addition to accounting for many of the commonly recognized local features of the text, Rader's hypothesis solves a number of critical controversies as well. For example, few critics of the book have avoided trying to account, in terms of the book's overall meaning, for the puzzling anomalies and discontinuities of the story and of Moll herself. She is not merely inconsistent. She seems ruled by no governing vision that would make a virtue even of inconsistency. What other critics see therefore as either novelistic confusion on Defoe's part—perhaps because the form is in its infancy—or thematic coherence—Defoe intends to present a picture of moral confusion—Rader argues is the natural consequence of imitating a true story. The adequacy of Rader's hypothesis finally depends on whether local effects produce an overall illusion of truth that of course would be at odds with the reader's external knowledge that the whole is a fiction. This question must wait until the texture of the episodes is examined.

Certainly much of Moll's attraction for readers lies in her evasiveness, her strange and frequently inconsistent strategies for dealing with a hostile world. One watches Moll as one watches his more interesting acquaintances, with a kind of puzzled fascination. No implied author helps to balance or reconcile her contradictions, her shifting mixture of assertiveness and indirection. She does not spring, it seems, from the same resources of imagination that spawned a Macbeth and would in time create a Clarissa and a Gwendolyn Harleth. Unlike Moll, these others exist so that one may finally come to understand and sympathize with their souls' confusions. Character, like every other significant element in a traditional dramatic or narrative action, serves as a complex set of signals indicating probable direction. Character, more importantly, serves as a constraint on meaning, on the reader's judgment. Clarissa's character does not exist for its own sake, although the success of the book does depend to a certain extent on the beauty of the finer brushstrokes. As a continuing and powerful semiological system, character both causes and results from complication, engendering both the basis of instability and the possibilities for its resolution. Moll's traits fail to become an intelligible "language," although because of their indeterminacy they can act as admirable departure points for any reader's private associational activities. Moll's personality therefore tends to float, to spurn any will to order inside her story. As a result, like the "future hero," Moll "may, according to the preoccupation of *each reader*, accommodate all sorts of comment—psychological, psychiatric, religious, or political." Yet, as an "indifferent Monitor," Moll refuses to yield to these "potentialities."[11] Interpretation fails to explain Moll, in the root sense of "make flat" and therefore observable at a glance. It must rather stretch her, raise some of Moll and lower other aspects in order that she may fit the critic's mold. Some, of course, would argue that it is criticism's treachery to blame, and this is partially true. Even so, a few examples of significant disjunction will show that Moll herself is the source of both pleasure and critical confusion.

Two contiguous episodes will serve nicely: Moll's near arrest for a theft she did not commit and the subsequent theft of the horse. In the first instance, Moll is for once falsely accused, dragged into a shop, "kept by force" (p. 241), and "barbarously" used (p. 243). Finally, some men who have pursued the real thief usher him into the shop. Recognizing a rare opportunity for a legal coup, Moll insists on appearing before a justice—a dangerous gambit, since her past exploits are so well known. The judge hears both sides, discharges Moll as the innocent party, and reprimands the accuser. He binds over the master and commits to Newgate the "Journeyman" who had most grievously insulted Moll. By "good Management," Moll and her attorney come off with "rather more" than two hundred pounds by threatening a suit (p. 252). This is Moll at her calculating best, adroit at the risky business of concealing her identity and past while at the same time manipulating an experienced tradesman into fearing an action Moll dare not bring. Then, "in good Circumstances indeed," with seven hundred pounds in money and a cache of stolen goods, far more than she would ever need to live comfortably, she sets out "not long after" this affair dressed "like a Beggar." An ill-chosen disguise, the "most uneasie" she ever donned, her clothes make it difficult even to approach a "gull." Yet she does meet with a "little Adventure." A drawer asks her to hold a horse while he attends to his master. Moll "takes the Horse, and walks off with him very soberly, and carri'd him" to her "Governess." Moll herself sees the "Robbery and no Robbery"—she cannot sell the horse, or take it to a stable—as "Ominous and Threatning" (p. 254).

How is the reader to take it? The very quality of fabrication, of patterning, that Robbe-Grillet condemns in the traditional novel, its ability to impose on the reader the values of the author, would dictate, if one were in a novelistic world, that this discrepancy function as a purposeful signal. Ordinary enough such moments may be in the real confusions of real people, nor is one often able to explain them. In the traditional novel disjunction must refer to probable developments. Take, for example, the most significant contradiction of a character like Lizzy Bennet: she prides herself on her discernment of character, recognizing immediately that Collins is unworthy both of her hand and her friend Charlotte's, yet she clearly forms too precipitously an unfavorable opinion of Darcy. Her good opinion of her own sagacity becomes therefore liable to shocking correction, leading to a deepened understanding of herself, and, within the comic probabilities of *Pride and Prejudice*, to a moral worthiness that then renders her a deserving candidate for fulfillment.

Moll's "muddle" seems at once to invite a simpler and demand a more complex response. Since the local experience of random truth is so powerful, one may accept as "like life" the juxtaposition of cunning with carelessness. After all, the most skillful confidence men are themselves sometimes "taken." One certainly cannot tell if irony is intended, unless one is willing to accept as "knowing" a conjecture about what Defoe "must" have believed. Were everyone the kind of naive, unanalytical reader Defoe probably thought he was writing for, one would probably respond with charmed but puzzled fascination, and go on avidly to the next episode. The history of the traditional novel interferes, however. As Ian Watt notes, two hundred years of reading authors "such as Jane Austen and Flaubert" who "incorporate such conflicts and incongruities into the very structure of their works" makes it difficult for any modern reader, even of the most plastic of imaginations, simply to "forget" the existence of a Defoe behind the mask.[12] Defoe *must* intend to mean, as did later authors that are also called novelists. Indeed, I have suggested that the potential for allusive generalization residing in Moll's portrayal stretches so widely that few can resist its blandishments. Moll's confusion then becomes an indication of approaching doom, since she can no longer distinguish safe from dangerous criminal activities. Or Moll seems, on the contrary, no hardened reprobate precisely because of this harmless, unthinking, almost comic sally. Lacking any strong system of represented belief but with over two centuries of traditonal fiction always bidding him to find meaning in inconsistency, the modern reader falls back on the last sanctuary of critical desperation: he creates the meaning he fails to find. Nourished on symbol and semantic complexity, yet thwarted by Defoe's literal paradigms, one must search elsewhere for what Defoe usually refuses to provide.

Except for obvious blunders, which are neither interesting nor critically significant, readers are prodded into repeated and various independent skirmishes with the text by these discrepancies and discontinuities. They range from clashes of episodes, as was just seen, to minor linguistic oddities. Almost as soon as one meets her, one may notice Moll's peculiar attitude toward the crime for which her mother was committed to Newgate. Moll says that her "Mother was convicted of Felony for a certain petty Theft, scarce worth naming, (*viz.*) Having an opportunity of borrowing three Pieces of fine *Hol-*

land, of a certain Draper in *Cheapside*" (p. 8). There is of course some doubt about the "Circumstances," so that Moll is uncertain "which is the right Account" (p. 8). This innocent passage presents virtually a model of the interpretive problems faced at every turn in *Moll Flanders*. How is one to judge Moll here? Some editors annotate "borrowing" to point out that Moll probably means, of course, "stealing." But that is little help. The diminutive force of "petty" and "scarce worth naming" clearly conflicts with the fact that what her mother stole was probably pretty valuable: *three* pieces of *fine* linen. If one imagines Moll as the writer of her own memoirs, spending the "Remainder" of her years "in sincere Penitence" with her dear "Jemmy," how can one countenance this casual attitude toward *meum* and *tuum*? "Borrowing" may now be used ironically to mean stealing, but I suspect most do not view the attitude as admirable, unless the act was indeed not stealing: "May I borrow a cigarette?" If Moll is not herself being ironic, what then becomes of her penitence? Or, is she indirectly condemning the brutality of a society that would punish with death such an objectively "petty" larceny? In that case, how does the message itself comment on Moll's later behavior? If the irony is Defoe's, at Moll's expense, then the sincerity of her repentance again is suspect. It would seem that the process by which an author's intuition becomes embodied in a form and then reproduced in the reader, as Croce describes it, has been blocked on both sides of the text. The reader can make all sorts of plausible conjectures about what Moll and her experience mean. Yet in doing so, it should be realized that one exercises powers authorized, not by the government of the text, but by one's individual right to create meaning where it literally does not exist.

Thus the "instruction" Defoe used to "Justifie the Publication" of Moll's "Private History" frequently has hard struggle to rise in our minds. Moll herself, of course, often points the lesson of her own behavior, but her "interpretations" of her own life are no more constrained than are her reader's. As moral geographer, she has abilities that are anything but awesome and her "muddle" has not escaped notice.[13] It is easy to conclude that Defoe did not himself recognize the difference between an appropriate generalization and one seriously askew.[14] But on one side of Moll is Crusoe and on the other Roxana. They do not always perceive their own inconsistencies, but when they do their remarks are usually perspicuous. Even so, for one so acute in her estimates of others, Moll's self-knowledge has wide gaps. For example, when she is still new in crime, Moll meets up with a little girl, leads her to a deserted passageway, encourages the child to prattle away, and steals her gold necklace. It occurs to Moll, as she stands there, to kill the child "that it might not Cry." She suddenly realizes that it must be "the Devil" who put into her mind this heinous thought, and she is so "frighted" by it that she is ready to "drop down." She feels what anyone, whose normal sensibilities had not been blunted by repeated acts of inhumanity, would feel. Yet there is no retrospective peroration of any kind on the horrors crime has led her to countenance. This "last Affair left no great Concern" upon Moll since, she says, "as I did the poor Child no harm, I only said to my self, I had given the Parents a just Reproof for their Negligence in leaving the poor little Lamb to come home by it self" (p. 194).

Whatever different values readers hold, they will still perceive something amiss here, a discrepancy not resolved by finding out that "casuistry" was a common deliberative mode in Defoe's time. No author steps in to reconcile the incommensurability of situation and commentary. Moll's "casuistry" is the problem, not the solution. Formally, a lively sense of personage may demand the juxtaposition of seemingly conflicting traits in order to suggest complexity. Yet complicating Moll, without any clear design to which complication is subordinate, tends to destroy the "simple" didacticism Defoe sometimes seems to desire. What is the "real" message of Moll's missing the deeper implications of her desire to kill? Is it that "Necessities" made her "regardless of any thing" (p. 194)? The convolutions of personality threaten to disappear beneath such "interpretation." Later writers would probably have tried to construct an instability out of these materials. Defoe is content to present them. One's judgment of Moll during such moments depends on no strong textual dictates, but on one's own differing naturalistic expectations about real people in the real world. One turns inward, if one questions Moll at all, for plausible explanations of her conflicting blindness and insight, since Defoe is silent.

The preface to *Moll Flanders* suggests that such moral ambiguity, the inadvertant result of writing an imitation of a true story, cannot have been intended in a book he asks readers to value more for the "Moral, than the Fable," the "Application" rather than the "Relation" (p. 2). Although the overall form of the book testifies to its fictionality, the continuing indeterminacy of episodes constitutes a liability a later novelist could not endure for a page. Perhaps no stretch of narrative is entirely free of redundancies, fissures, uncompleted thoughts, missed or ill-conceived designs, from all sorts of usurpations or deflections of the text's frail unity. Yet some novelists manage, by violence or cunning, to yoke their recalcitrant materials to a single purpose, the imposition of form on the fluctuating moments of experience. Moll's story has entirely different virtues, although many readers would not exchange her fascinating mutations for all of Fielding's benevolent and perspicuous tyranny. Nevertheless, whether one conceives of the novelist's art as sweetened communication or significant talespinning, something is lost when one cannot know how to judge Moll. Defoe, like the "new" novelist, pays the price no neoclassical author would willingly pay: an impairment of his ability to sway his readers' minds.

Even so, moral ambiguity in *Moll Flanders* does not equal an illusion of literal truth, equivalent to the *Memoirs* and the *Journal*. All it indicates is an absence of any continuous controlling presence, one that functions on every page. Indeed, Moll and her story contain and exist in much that is negative space. Yet the book still manages to tell the reader that it is a fiction. "The one impossible event," Woolf says of Moll, "is that she should settle down in comfort and security."[15] At any time that one can say something cannot happen in a narrative one is on the trail of a converse principle of generation and selection. What it might be for Moll's story cannot be seen until one examines in some detail the differences between the ways fiction and auto- biography are conceived. The obvious answer is only partially satis- factory: first-person novels, no matter how closely based on actual events, are self-contained. As interesting as it may be to discover real people standing just behind Hemingway's characters, the reader does not have to know of them to participate fully in the experience and significance of the story.

Real memoirs and diaries, on the other hand, have a referential relationship to the events they purport to relate, even, paradoxically, if readers are not familiar with those events. For this reason is the power of the *Journal* historical: there must have been a 1665 plague in London. Perhaps all narrative finally involves illusion, since it attempts to represent something in words that is not itself words. It is known, however, that some kinds of narrative, satire for example, force the reader to construe their matter as referring outward. *Gulliv- er's Travels* is peremptory in this regard, at least in many passages. When Gulliver says that "Flimnap, the Treasurer, is allowed to cut a Caper on the strait Rope, at least an Inch higher than any other Lord in the whole Empire," the reader may not have the slightest inkling that for Flimnap one is meant to read Walpole. Yet the reader knows that Flimnap equals someone. That inference is necessary if the book is to be anything more than a charming bit of nonsense. This sense of reference, or representing something that has existed or yet exists in heaven or on the earth, is not automatically eradicated by the imposition on materials of an illusion of "madeness." Paul Fussell has noted just such qualities in First War memoirs, and argues that it assimilates them to the novel.[16] Rearrangements of chronology, transformations of events, manipulations of personae—all the devices of treatment as opposed to substance—may point to the gray area where fiction and history might meet.

But the intention to write neither novel nor memoir precludes such aesthetic accommodations. Since works that are easily recognized as one or the other are written with some regularity, something else must be involved. The distinction is precisely in use, the "for the sake of what" involved in all human productions. In the real memoir, decisions involving the "telling" are made for the sake of the subject, the "I," conceived of as the author's own public personality. Concealment, changes in the story's clock time, any sort of rhetoric, broadly conceived, occur to assist the memorialist in recording his own personality in words that convey his reality. The effect, although only to be achieved in the mind of a reader, is understood as an aspect of the writer. In the first-person novel, on the contrary, experiments with both matter and technique occur to realize effects conceived of as in the reader, although the novel's form is the sign system in which the potential effect is embedded. Anyone who has ever tried to write much fiction knows the radical difference between these two modes. The fabulist asks, among other things, not how better to reveal himself, but how to achieve the desired effect.

Yet this clear distinction is blurred by *Moll Flanders*. Defoe intends the local episode to be taken as the product of a naive diarist, while at the same time the overall form reveals a mimetic intention not Moll's. What signals authorship other than the narrator's is neither referentiality nor verisimilitude, but selection designed to make possible a continuum of pleasure and significance ordinarily available only sporadically in real memoirs. While the separate episodes contain an implicit request that the reader conceive of Moll as nothing other than the reporter of her own experiences, the book as a whole requires that one view it as an epitome. The book's positive fictional principle coexists, uneasily, with the firmest local sense of truth. The same anomaly is at work in *Robinson Crusoe*, but not in any systematic and purposeful manner. Sequences exist that give the strongest impression of elements specified for an effect, within an overall structure that imitates the expressive intention of autobiographical documents. What I have called novelistic moments in Crusoe's story, mimetic "outcroppings," will not easily be encompassed by a general expressive illusion. It is not surprising that Starr cannot make the autobiographical model he designed to explain the subsuming expressive illusion of *Robinson Crusoe* fit the virtually opposite relationship of episodes to overall intention in *Moll Flanders*. Now it can also be seen why Rader, working within a framework that assumes parts are subordinate to the whole, would emphasize the illusory expressiveness of the book at the expense of its qualities of purposeful design. One has seen too much fictional patterning, the other too little.

By his choice of what not to represent, Defoe signals that his heroine is indeed a creation and not the naive autobiographer that the reader's continuing encounters with her try to confirm. She never develops anything like the tight, causal relationships with other people that are necessary for the probabilities of the novel to occur. Even so, the potentialities for such an interlocking are frequently present, as in her first romantic involvement and her later doings with her "Jemmy." It is of course not sufficient that she reencounters Jemmy later on. Novelistic character requires that human interaction result either as a cause or an effect of a systematic narrative syntax. Given sufficient time and paper, Defoe could have had Moll meet up with everyone she had ever known before and he still would not have written a novelistic action—although some of the randomness of Moll's adventures would thereby have disappeared.

Her story progresses, rather, by a principle of avoiding such regularity. At any time she finds herself "the happiest Creature alive" (p. 85), she ceases, not necessarily to be interesting as a potential novelistic character, but as a chronicler of wondrous episodes no real memoir could ever match. Calm stability usually terminates abruptly and, for the story at hand, conveniently: "an odd and surprizing Event put an end to all that Felicity in a moment." Moll is left "the most uncomfortable, if not the most miserable" creature "in the World," all the more eligible for her next adventure (p. 86). Defoe may even include a précis to call to mind just how delicious previous entanglements have been and therefore how much there is to look forward to: "Then it occurr'd to me what an abominable Creature am

I! and how is this innocent Gentleman going to be abus'd by me! How little does he think, that having Divorc'd a Whore, he is throwing himself into the Arms of another! that he is going to Marry one that has lain with two Brothers, and has had three Children by her own Brother! one that was born in *Newgate*, whose Mother was a Whore, and is now a transported Thief; one that has lain with thirteen Men, and has had a Child since he saw me!" (p. 182). Periodically, the slate is wiped clean: "I was now a single Person again, *as I may call my self*, I was loos'd from all the Obligations either of Wedlock or Mistressship in the World; except my Husband the Linnen Draper, who . . . no Body could blame me for thinking my self entirely freed from" (p. 126). Within a short time of marrying Moll, the new husband loses his money, then "grew Melancholy and Disconsolate, and from thence Lethargick, and died" (p. 189).

Defoe declines to represent stretches of secure happiness, but not because such scenes are not novelistically promising. The history of the traditional novel is in part the process of finding more and more of interest in just such "inert" moments of life. But *Moll Flanders* is not a traditional novel. It is a fictional refinement of real memoirs. Veritable chronicles of self can proceed by means of the same lopped episodes that Defoe employs, by means of extended analyses of the nuances of every moment, or, more commonly, by means of some unsystematic combination of the two. The paradox of Moll's story is that the quality of the next episode can always be predicted, with even more certainty than in the traditional novel, but the probable content can never be known. Whatever happens next in Moll's "life," it is sure to be sufficiently bizarre to hold the reader's interest: a kidnapping by gypsies; a seduction by one brother followed by marriage to the other; another marriage, this time to her own brother; marriage again, to a man who thinks Moll has a fortune, and leaves her, reluctantly, when he finds out she does not; the difficulties of a pregnant Moll, alone and husbandless—and on and on. Literal verisimilitude of the sort found in the *Journal* and the *Memoirs* requires the inclusion of an occasional episode that reasserts the reality of the life just by showing how uninteresting a full report of it can sometimes be. Moll's life is never intentionally unsensational, although her manner of relation frequently is.

Another important modification of the factual tradition, a refinement of possibilities present in *Robinson Crusoe*, does not force itself on the reader if local effects are examined: Moll's role as narrator. Of course, she is vividly represented, although her personality frequently changes in unexpected ways under the pressures of succeeding episodes. Her point of view, however, never deviates, a consistency she shares only with Roxana. Events are always seen through the central, pervasive "I," to a degree no mere pronoun can convey. Unlike Crusoe, Jack, and, it goes without saying, H.F. and the Cavalier, Moll never simply reports what she sees for its own intrinsic interest. She melts the world down and recasts it in the mold of her own personality. Crusoe, before and after his island isolation, recedes into the background in order to describe what in some ways never lost primacy: the world outside his mind. In such a narrative strategy, which is also a kind of authorial vision, experience is not conceived of as psychological and changing. It is a static "other," existing externally and therefore capable of being communicated only if the idiosyncratic self is kept from meddling. The future of the novel, quite obviously, waited behind other doors, to be unlocked only by discoveries leading to greater revelation of personality, not its muting. *Moll Flanders* is one such discovery, even though the ubiquity of the beholding consciousness is itself encompassed by the superficial illusion of truth. The advance had to be made, and some have equated it with the rise of the novel. Indeed, Moll seems so much more vivid than earlier narrators not just because of the much-praised paraphernalia of realism—many earlier pseudomemoirs used similar strategies of internal confirmation—but because Defoe refuses to dilute the intensity of her focus. Vividness is not, however, identical to the traditional novel.

Even at those moments when Moll seems to pull back and observe, her personality merely bides its time until it can integrate the scene into the internal landscape.

One Adventure I had which was . . . I was going thro' *Lombard-street* in the dusk of the Evening, just by the end of *Three King Court*, when on a sudden comes a Fellow running by me as swift as Lightning, and throws a Bundle that was in his Hand just behind me, as I stood up against the corner of the House at the turning into the Alley; just as he threw it in he said, God bless you Mistress let it lie there a little, and away he runs swift as the Wind: After him comes two more, and immediately a young Fellow without his Hat, crying stop Thief, and after him two or three more, they pursued the two last Fellows so close, that they were forced to drop what they had got, and one of them was taken into the bargain, the other got off free.

I Stood stock still all this while till they came back, dragging the poor Fellow they had taken, and luging the things they had found, extremely well satisfied that they had recovered the Booty, and taken the Thief; and thus they pass'd by me, for I look'd only like one who stood up while the Crowd was gone.

Once or twice I ask'd what was the matter, but the People neglected answering me, and I was not very importunate. [p. 195]

If Moll seems here to be merely an observer, the context of the passage reveals something quite different. She has just robb'd the child of the gold necklace. She then goes on to say, "I had a great many Adventures after this, but I was young in the Business, and did not know how to manage, otherwise than as the Devil put things into my Head. . . . One Adventure I had which was . . . ," and then follows the scene I have quoted at length. After Moll's wry comment that she was not very "importunate," she continues, "but after the Crowd was wholly pass'd, I took my opportunity to turn about and take up what was behind me and walk away: This indeed I did with less Disturbance"—to her conscience, that is—"for these things I did not steal, but they were stolen to my Hand" (p. 196). This thinking involves the "casuistry" Starr finds at the heart of Moll's meditations, but it also displays the pervasive manner in which the external world is transformed by Moll's mind into corrolaries of her own hopes and fears. Moments of such connection are scattered throughout Defoe's narratives. Only in *Moll Flanders* and *Roxana* are they a unifying device, albeit an unobtrusive one. The traditional novel finally came to feed on such relationships, character implying event and the reverse. Even so, Moll's interactions yield no pattern, nothing of the ongoing and progressive synthesis necessary for the novel to come. The material is present, the technique would not now be a radical shift for Defoe, but yet no novelistic world emerges. Instead, Moll's story is a series of varying, fascinating portraits of the shifting landscape of a mind at work on the materials of survival.

The simplest test of this hypothesis would be to ask what response that Moll might make to her adventitious "Bundle" would seem inappropriate, given the book's internal geometry: leaving it out of fear; picking it up, but recognizing that her act was still theft; joyfully possessing it without even a consideration of the ethical question; or something else? No standard of exclusion within the book rules these or other possible responses anomalous, although any single reader might say, "No, that's not the Moll *I* know." The only "necessity" is that Moll link events to her psyche and situation. Her ubiquity provides an important building block for the house of the novel, but as yet there exists no blueprint.

I have been talking for the most part about the tacit experience that results from Defoe's duality of purpose, but the specifiable meaning of *Moll Flanders*, to the extent that it contains and does not merely suggest ideas, arises from this same source. Defoe's aim finally is ironic, though not in any ordinary sense. Within an overall structure based on the refinement of effects possible in true stories, he enfolds episodes that reveal enticing, often bewildering, ambiguity. As in the compound sentence, where either coordinate clause can precede, so too in *Moll Flanders* can local elements be rearranged, with no violence done to the overall structure. One half of this paradox does not challenge explanation. Although, as Stewart says, "illusion had become the sine qua non for aesthetic enjoyment of serious fiction" in the previous century, by the time Defoe writes, the necessity for the ruse had diminished.[17] It is too strong to say that fiction had suddenly gained respectability; even in 1740 Richardson pretends he merely edits Pamela's letters. More likely, illusionists such as Defoe probably tired of the strong constraints the pseudomemoir imposed on experimentation. Little manipulation of the author-reader relationship, the source of so many innovations in narrative over the next two centuries, could be attempted when the narrator had to seem to be the author. The shift from event-centered narrative, no matter how many undetectable liberties Defoe might take with the materials of the *Journal* or the *Memoirs*, to the representation of personality was a drastic change, and one Defoe clearly did not always find palatable. Creation has a way of interfering with the didactic tidiness he says he valued. The Horatian ideal proves efficacious only when authors employ unambiguous, highly coded, even stylized forms to serve as carriers of lucid commentary, social or moral wisdom, as Johnson knew. The writer who essays a new species of writing risks not being understood, as novelists as diverse as Fielding, Sterne, Emily Brontë, Joyce, and Camus have discovered. It is no accident that Johnson attempted no realistic fiction in which the world, as in Moll's tale, is "promiscuously described." The mimetic impulse can run counter to Johnson's belief that "where historical veracity has no place," fabulists should represent only "the most perfect idea of virtue."[18] How could an author like Defoe, who for so many years had thought of himself as a kind of public conscience, avoid feeling a certain uneasiness if a created personality began to take on life of her own?

At any rate, in outfitting Moll with a life and opinions, Defoe leaves behind all but the most commonplace of his own beliefs. With sufficient knowledge of his ideas expressed in other places, one can easily track Defoe in *Moll Flanders*. Moll quotes the "wise Man's Prayer, Give me not Poverty least I steal" (p. 191). As Starr discovered, Defoe argues the same view of necessity and crime in the *Review* and *The Compleat English Gentleman*. Once Moll has been sentenced to death, she begins to "look back upon" her "past Life with abhorrence." Faced with eternity, it seemed "the greatest stupidity in Nature to lay any weight upon" this life. Again, as Starr notes in his edition of the book, Defoe has anticipated this otherworldly view in

"A Vision of the Angelick World."[19] On nearly every page, Starr finds Moll iterating Defoe. What is finally notable about this mass of opinions—Starr's *Moll Flanders* is the most heavily annotated Defoe narrative in the Oxford series—is that they could be of abiding interest only to the historian of moral commonplaces.

Few of Defoe's ideas are particularly dissentient or even original, certainly as contrasted with the innovation of his narrative experiments. Despite Novak's desire to show that Defoe has been unjustly "condemned for shallow content and a paucity of moral perception," he must finally concede that Defoe "was neither an original nor a profound thinker."[20] It is undoubtedly distorting to single out, from a study that bases its conclusion on such an admirable breadth of reading, just one of Novak's examples: "Although Defoe's use of necessity [in *Moll Flanders* and *Roxana*] as an excuse for theft followed the theories established by the seventeenth-century civilians, his extension of this same doctrine to prostitution seems to have been without precedent." Neither shallow nor profound, one yet wonders how such stale ideologies could possibly be the cause of Defoe's continuing popularity. The history of ideas approach to Defoe seems to have left us with a pale, washed-out retailer of tired truisms, instead of the vital, engaged explorer of uncharted narrative ground I think Defoe was. The very facility with which Defoe's hackneyed opinions come tumbling out of Moll's mind indicates, not that they are the heart of the book, but that he assigns plausible beliefs to Moll at any point her personality seems to call for generalization. To argue, therefore, that "we cannot understand the morality of Defoe's 'moral romance'" if we have not painstakingly acquired "a knowledge of natural law"—or, someone might similarly argue, Defoe's political or economic ideas—seems to me special pleading, an implicit denial that most readers have a sound basis for their liking Defoe, as well as a drastic simplification of the often indirect ways belief can operate in narrative. After so many attempts to find semantic complexity in Defoe have turned up so little that is indeed complex, might it not be time to look elsewhere for his power to endear generations of readers?[21]

Finally, since Defoe's unquestionable talent seemed to be storytelling, and since stories, by their very nature, mean as a function of their teleologies, the locus of Defoe's beliefs in *Moll Flanders* may be elusive if one pays overmuch attention to the inveterately conventional utterances of Moll herself. It is Moll's *story* that means, much more than her opinions, just as it is the working out, by coincidence, of Tom Jones's fate, rather than Fielding's ideas about the necessity for prudence in the world, that is the central meaning of Fielding's novel. As a creator of human situations, Defoe is far more profound than any of the separate ideas he assigns his characters. This disjunction indicates, of course, that Defoe has not yet evolved anything like a novelistic technique to subordinate belief to a system of character and action. Novak recognized the liability: "although Defoe's preoccupation with natural law enriches the content of his fiction, it also tends to destroy some of his excellence as a creator of character."[22] Novak has it just backwards, I would argue: it is Moll's personality that "enriches" the triteness of the ideological content. Yet the relationship is, as Novak implies, additive.

One important problem in the study of narrative today is meaning, as so many European critics, like Todorov, fully understand. It may finally be understood, with the help of writers like Defoe, that meaning does not arise in a single way, as Sheldon Sacks suggested fifteen years ago.[23] Perhaps the surest way to guarantee that the question of meaning remains unanswered is to continue to employ a critical method that assumes an author's beliefs can simply be extracted from what the characters say or inferred in some easy way from what they do. Defoe's fate, to be interpreted into triteness, perhaps awaits any author treated by such a method. The tough-minded Fielding, for example, can thereby be made into a kind of mild Sunday school teacher admonishing his charges to love one another better, if only one conveniently forgets that, within the world of *Tom Jones*, it is not virtue that is rewarded but luck. The even more inexorable Swift, in the hands of critics who ignore Gulliver's status as a device for ridicule, begins to sound like some "humane" satirist who disowns his narrator's final misanthropic vision. He really was insincere when he said, "*Mundum odi.*"[24] The very choice of how views will be incorporated into narrative often reveals more about an author than the beliefs one can "pull" from the living texture of the story, a lesson Conrad should long ago have taught everyone. The enduring power of *Moll Flanders* resides, not in its messages, but in Moll's existence. She, and Defoe's other narrators, despite their social and legal transgressions, recommend all the conventionalisms of polite society—trade, monarchy, property, public morality—and of the spiritual life—faith, grace, God's mercy—with an explicit confidence hardly mystifying. One needs such beliefs in a society such as Defoe's, which cared little for the dignity or even safety of the individual.

So the formal paradox implicit in the structure of *Moll Flanders* extends to its meaning as well, since the conventionality of Defoe's heroine is belied by the kind of story she tells. Defoe had once said, "Mankind are Rogues by Birth." Yet that easy homily, inherited, as Novak says, from the tradition of natural law, had long since been superseded by a bitter personal knowledge, learned in betrayal, in hiding from friend and foe alike.[25] The chaos of human relationships is of course reflected in the episodic subject matter of the book, but it also controls the episodic manner of relation, the refusal to subsume the confusion to any strong system. The formal development of his narratives, the movement from loose pseudofactual structures in which he embodies his more general and less powerfully personal ideas to more novelistic teleologies, is paralleled by a growing desire and ability to represent the chaos from which he had suffered. The "refinement" of *Moll Flanders*, in which such moments of noncommunication are not only collected, but prevented from casting mutual light on the surrounding ones, mirrors the attempt to make sense of the world that is in part the story of Defoe's narrative development. This is not to commit the "fallacy of imitative form" or the "ancient reductive fallacy of identifying the thoughts of characters with those of their author," of seeing Moll, Jack, and Roxana as just so many projections of Defoe's personality.[26] Almost the opposite is true. Defoe stands back from Moll and creates her whole. Yet, even though she is a product of his imagination, and not of an act of impersonation, he has not achieved the same thing as an immanent presence that would make of his beliefs, especially his less sanguine ones, positively functioning elements. The discontinuity of human life is implied by the disjunctions of *Moll Flanders*, but it is not literally represented; the form is not imitative of his profound beliefs. Not until *Roxana* will he find a way to manipulate the materials and techniques of fiction so as to create traditional novelistic meaning, or what will become traditional long after he is dead. The moral indeterminacy of Moll, as expressive as it is, took Defoe away from the traditional novel.

V

Novelistic Possibilities

"IT IS JUST THE POET'S FREEDOM," remarks Murray Krieger, "to put teleology where his object of imitation had none that distinguishes him from even the most arrogant historian who would fashion the past in the shapes of his private fancy." The process of converting "the empirical world's *casual* into art's *causal*" may indeed be a kind of liberation, especially for an author like Defoe.[1] Yet it is also an exacting kind of creative activity requiring artistic intuition of a sort Defoe would not have encountered evidence of outside the drama or epic. Later novelists would routinely attempt to endow their stories with progressive powers since that structure came to be equivalent to the novel. Despite the suspense of *Tom Jones*, it is always unthinkable that Tom will fulfill the prophecy that "he was certainly born to be hanged." Indeed, it is obvious that he will be rewarded, although Fielding's narrator constantly reiterates *he*, and not a world in which justice reigns, is responsible. The coordinate structure of *Moll Flanders* establishes expectations of much less force: Moll will be the center of each episode, her adventures will be fascinating, and everything that happens to her will, as Rader notes, strike the reader as spectacular either in treatment or nature. The usual will appear the bizarre and vice versa. Even so, the casual reigns, as a function of the sequence's additive principle of being.

Yet even in *Moll Flanders* moments of novelistic potential surface, episodes that, if Defoe had not always so ruthlessly cut them short, could have lent themselves to complication and resolution. One such moment was seen in *Robinson Crusoe*. Others occur in *Colonel Jack*, where Defoe works, by fits and stops, toward the arrangements of subject and technique he will need in *Roxana*. One example from *Moll Flanders* seems in order, if only to show how completely the governing form of the book dictates the annihilation of such situations.

The similarities between Moll and Richardson's Pamela have not escaped readers. Moll is cast adrift on the world, finally landing with a poor but respectable woman who makes her living by boarding orphans. Through contact with a few of the town's gentry and their daughters, Moll becomes "very Mannerly," a "Gentlewoman indeed," at least according to her own definition, able to gain her bread with her needle. "At last," at a time when Moll is "not a little Proud," one "of the Ladies" takes her home for a month "to be among her Daughters" (pp. 14–15). Just as for Pamela, living with her "good lady," this opportunity means benefits unavailable to a young woman who otherwise would be condemned to the kitchen or, worse, the workhouse. Such elevation, however, at the same time threatens both Moll and Pamela with some perilous possibilities. As Moll's "old good Woman" contends, raising Moll above her station could "do the little Gentlewoman more harm than good" (p. 15). She means, quite reasonably, that "Genteel living" can so affect an impressionable child that she is no longer "so easie" in her "old Quarters" (p. 16); worse, she can accidentally be prepared for a life of ease inevitably unattainable. Moll continues to live in "smooth" circumstances, growing up a "very Handsome" girl, of a "Character" very "sober, modest, and vertuous," although it is a virtue untested by the wiles of men or the vagaries of fortune (p. 19).

Here is a situation similar to the one with which Richardson commences *Pamela*, eighteen years later. Of course Richardson compresses into Pamela's first letter information that Moll gives over many pages, but that simply reveals Richardson's different aims and greater economy of technique. The reader learns immediately that Pamela is "qualified above her degree" and that her "young master" is more than innocently interested in her. One knows, that is, as a result of the causal relationship established between characters, and between them and the developing situation, that Pamela will be faced with certain choices, on which her economic and moral fate will depend. Will she "return back to be a clog" on her "dear parents," or stain her virtue, or what? The pattern, as Sheldon Sacks and more recently, Rader have explained, develops "along a line of branching alternatives, where one branch, always closed by circumstances or choice, leads to an ethically acceptable but materially undesirable safety"—returning home, marrying Williams—"while the other leads overtly and immediately to greater danger"—rape, or suicide— "but covertly and ultimately to the most desirable resolution of her difficulties"—marriage to Squire B.[2] This instability so permeates the book that it continues to exert its force even after the marriage would seem to have resolved it. The same traits of character and the same social conditions that complicated the situation require the story's continuance, the consequences of a bright, pretty, but impoverished girl marrying a headstrong, selfish, and wealthy raconteur in a society inclined to despise and ridicule unequal "love matches."

Defoe creates similar expectations about Moll. Her virtue will be tested and she will face choices implying happiness or misery, moral as well as material. For such a sequence to work novelistically, and there is no reason why it should, it must develop along the lines of a continuing instability. Instead, Moll loses her virtue posthaste and Defoe then involves her in an entirely different situation, also of novelistic potential, but based on considerations now having little to do with her volition. Seduced by the older brother, Moll finds herself the object of honorable intentions by the younger. Clearly, Defoe is thinking in terms of placing Moll in as many situations of conflict as he can invent, although the novelistic tendencies of her "bind" at this point could still be developed, along with a great deal of corollary suspense. Instead, Moll simply agrees, after "an Hour and Half" of "Discourse" with the elder brother, to marry the other brother. The marriage lasts five years, but since it "concerns the Story in hand very little," she passes over the period in a page. She then embarks on the series of adventures, matrimonial, adulterous, and felonious, that move the book even farther away from novellike effects. Clearly Defoe has been more interested in the fact of Moll's marrying her seducer's brother than in the possible instability residing in the situation. It is this quality of epitomized sensationalism that draws so many readers to Moll's story. But it is a fictional method in which the anomalies of life seem to have few important consequences. Moll, it is often remarked, is untouched by her travails. Yet novelistic characters *must* be affected, else there can be no instability.

Even within these two sequences from Moll's early career, little sense of the probable, with which one associates many forms of the traditional novel, ever develops. In novels such as *Pride and Prejudice* and *A Farewell to Arms*, personality, event, and ideology interact to suggest likely outcome. Suspense there is, but it is in the working out of a character's fate. The linkage in *Moll Flanders* remains casual or, one might say, historical: this is how it happens in real life, where probability is a chimera. Moll's decisions do not entail inevitability, and indeed, such a sense would conflict with the radical discontinuity of human affairs Defoe represents. The sustained control vital to a continuing instability is missing and one wonders if Defoe would have employed it, as he does in *Roxana*, even if he had recognized the possibilities. Although it is wrong to argue that Defoe was "destitute of the power to fathom any intricacies of human nature,"[3] he is primarily concerned with Moll's solitary life and its disjunctive consequences in her behavior and psyche.

Defoe steadfastly resists the novelistic blandishments of his next story as well, *Colonel Jack*.[4] The book begins with the most vivid and extended portrait of inner life in Defoe, one on which critics have heaped praise. Even so, it is if anything even less novelistic than the opening of *Moll Flanders*. Jack, another orphan who, like Captain

Bob, has no one to guide him through the temptations of an impoverished childhood, finally falls into thievery. "A poor innocent Boy"
with "no evil" in his "Intentions," he has never "stolen any thing"
until falling in with a "new Instructor," who teaches him the tricks of
the trade (p. 19). Though recognizing that he is "ripening a-pace for
the Gallows . . . in the high Road to the Devil" and that such a life
contradicts his desire to be a "Gentleman," these reflections always
"wore off again, as often as they came on" and he "follow'd the old
Trade again" (p. 62). Such a pattern virtually precludes any sort of
progressive action, since the reader sees a post facto iteration of
consequences and not a representation of how they came about. What
occasionally seem to be tendencies toward a kind of action of "better-
ment," in which Jack will achieve his goals of gentility, are balked
because Jack's traits and volition are not the cause of what Jack
becomes. His final economic security, initiated by discovering a way
to control, with "kindness," the "illnatured ungovernable Negroes"
(p. 150), his master's slaves, results only as an adventitious outcome
of circumstances. The same could be said of Tom Jones's final success,
of course. Even so, Fielding's plot still lets the reader know that
reward is probable and that Tom deserves to be rewarded. Character
contributes both to complication and resolution. Jack's career consists of being "removed by the degrees that you have heard from a
Pick-pocket, to a Kidnapp'd miserable Slave in *Virginia* . . . then
from a Slave to a Head Officer, and Overseer of Slaves, and from
thence to a Master Planter" (pp. 151–152). This summary, like
Moll's similar one, reminds the reader that he is in an epitome of
wonders. It also betokens Defoe's ad hoc rejection of novelistic
teleology. The example of Fielding suggests that the novelist can
represent *causal* sequences only to suggest how chaotic life is com-
pared to art, how unlikely in the real world Tom's pleasing success
would be. But even though Fielding's beliefs—in part a reaction to
the naiveté of Richardson's "virtue rewarded"—may be negative, he
still expresses them in a form possessing the positive power of
structured experience. While Defoe's refusal to dramatize his own

presence in his narratives may, as I have suggested, imply a view of the world, it does not effectively express it by means of an ongoing causal agency. His narratives do not, as wholes, attain that philosophical density Aristotle noted was a feature of causally plotted mimesis.

Even so, *Colonel Jack* contains a clear model for the concluding novelistic sequence of *Roxana*. As in the later work, it involves a threat from the past just at the point happiness at last seems in reach. With Jack's "Fortunes" finally "settled for this World" in an "Estate more than sufficient," with not "the least apprehensions of any Evil breaking out," an "unseen Mine blew up" all his "apparent Tranquility" (pp. 263–264). As in *Roxana*, the narrator, after summarizing the disturbing and unexpected consequences, "must now return" to a part of his "History" that "had been past for some Time" (p. 264). Not only does Defoe thereby commit himself to a chronological shift, a rarity in itself, he also forges a relationship between past perceptions and actions and present consequences. In life, such connections may seldom occur unambiguously; in the novel, they are a staple. Jack, it seems, once sallied out to join the Pretender's Jacobite supporters in the uprising of "the '15," even though his wife, "Moggy," had begged him to rest easy at home. Earlier, Jack had said he had "sat still and look'd on, for which" he later "had Reason to be thankful" (p. 250). Apparently he did not tell the full truth. Now we learn that he had given his wife "the Slip" after a "*Romish* Priest" had "inspir'd" him "with new Zeal" (p. 264). The indecision, as usual, probably is Defoe's. At any rate, the threat now arises from some transported rebels arriving in the vicinity of Jack's plantation. He continues awhile terrified of some disastrous revelation that will blast all his hopes.

Clearly Defoe has here the raw materials for a suspenseful sequence. The shift in time even affords him, as it will in *Roxana*, an opportunity to bind his materials tightly into a unity, local as it might be. Yet Defoe does little with these possibilities. The threat quickly diminishes as Jack's wife provides the "Direction" for Jack to extricate himself from "this Labrinth" (p. 268). Why worry when a pardon from London is easily bought? Jack goes away so that no one will discover him until the pardon arrives, has a successful trading voyage—Defoe's solution to Jack's problem indicates that the entire episode was conceived, not for its own vital sake, but to get Jack to sea again—and finally receives word that "his Majesty had resolv'd . . . to grant a general Pardon" (p. 275). Even this news comes as a kind of narrative afterthought, since Defoe's attention has since wandered elsewhere, to the capitalistic possibilities of illicit trade with Spanish Mexico. While Jack felt threatened, however, while the possibilities still loomed for being "discover'd, betray'd, carried to *England*, hang'd, quarter'd, and all that was terrible" (p. 269), Defoe had on his hands something with novelistic potential. As in Crusoe's fear of the cannibals, the threat productive of such complications would have turned on external matters and not psychological necessity—Jack feels no remorse at being a traitor. At stake may be his "Plantations" and "Estate," even his neck, but not his soul or even his heart. The ethical components of an instability, Defoe will learn with Roxana, must vibrate more closely to the centers of his narrators' beings.

Crusoe starved for companionship, Moll yearning to be a "Gentle-woman," Jack fearing a chance recognition—these are novelistic moments imbedded in the additive continuity of episodic time. Defoe does not develop them for two primary reasons. His desire to maintain local randomness makes them a liability, since they violate historicity with their telic purposefulness. Second, the creation of a continuing instability requires not just an appropriate situation but also a set of skills Defoe would not have found in previous narrative, although they were available in the drama. Defoe finally discovered, unmistakably by accident, a novelistic situation he could not ignore in Roxana's precarious security threatened by her daughter. The intuitive power that makes the conclusion of *Roxana* the first extended novelistic action in well-known English fiction must have come from deeper imaginative springs than Defoe was accustomed to tapping.

"Roxana": The Novel Becoming

Many critics have suggested that Defoe achieved some sort of innovation with his last major fictional narrative, *Roxana, the Fortunate Mistress.* Alan D. McKillop remarked that "Defoe is probably getting into a tighter story than he had bargained for" but avoided "going on to the full development of the catastrophe." Bonamy Dobrée thought that, had Defoe "been able to carry it through," *Roxana* "might have constituted another step forward in the art." More recently, Robert D. Hume has noted an "essential cohesiveness," a "brilliantly designed whole," and Wallace Jackson, going even further, argued that, in *Roxana*, to "some very large extent, Defoe was the first to define and to explore that area of representation in which the British novel was to realize some of its most marked successes."[5]

These insights seem to me soundly based on accurate perceptions of Defoe's accomplishment. There is something new about *Roxana*. It is a departure from Defoe's ordinary method. Yet the same understandable desire to assimilate Defoe to later, more traditional, developments in prose fiction, a desire that leads to seeing his earlier works as coherent novels, seems again to be at work here to grant *Roxana* more novelistic coherence than it possesses. In so doing, the reader not only misses the nature of Defoe's accomplishment but also tends to overlook how many small modifications of older traditions had to occur before the revolutionary form of the novel could be born. Most of *Roxana* differs very little in structure from his earlier works, although the subject, as many have noted, is much darker, a brooding study of sin, guilt, and retribution. It is only in the extended conclusion of the book that Defoe departs from his normal mode and heads in a direction that, if later novelists like Richardson and Fielding had known more about Defoe, would have provided the novel with an instructive antecedent.

This innovation involves not just subject and treatment, but the entire way a fictional world is made to signify. It is a synthesis more important than any single element in the alchemical transformation. Once Defoe shifts the normal chronology of the story, a shift few have noticed and no one has adequately understood, and goes back to show how Roxana's daughter brought her "in danger," one can see emerging possibilities for the nascent forms that came to be known as the novel.[6] Roxana ceases to be just a highly developed collocation of fascinating but divergent traits and becomes a consistent character. The events of the story cease to be a mere string and take on the working power of a plot, an instability that demands completion, as indicated at least in part by the conclusion being the longest stretch of continuous narration in Defoe. Finally, as a function of the causal nature of that plot, one can have an *anticipatory* experience; one perceives in advance the nature of a promised fate for a character, which may justly be called tragic.[7] The new demands on Defoe result in a story that now demands more from the reader.

To call *Roxana*, or at least its conclusion, tragic indicates that finally Defoe has adapted a pattern distinctly nonnarrative to his own purposes. Roxana, it is true, hardly conforms to normal expectations of what tragic heroines should be, although plenty of evidence exists that Defoe tries to "elevate" her stature. In the difficulties he has— they are not perfectly solved—Defoe struggles with another important problem, aside from the creation of novelistic structure: *Roxana* is one of the earliest examples in the as yet unwritten history of how "the soul of tragedy transmigrated from drama to narrative," a process that continues to provide examples today.[8] Defoe's guilt-ridden courtesan, despite her final wealth, is the first in a long line of middle-class tragic or pathetic figures whose stories demand the internal view narrative affords. Defoe had previously employed his narrators for radically differing purposes. As reporter or personage, each narrator was conceived to satisfy requirements on the level of the episode, sometimes even of the subepisodic moment. For this reason I have insisted on the distinction between personage and character. At the inception of her story, Roxana is a personage, not a character; not until the conclusion does she begin to demand from Defoe an integrative method. Character is not just a matter of consistency, it is pattern put to use in order to convey probable fate. Roxana's past becomes determinative of the present, which then becomes another determinative past. This final sequence of *Roxana* signals not only a new kind of story, but a new attitude toward the purpose of stories.

I do not mean to suggest that *Roxana* is a consummately happy success. It finally lacks something both as novel and as tragedy. Even so, by virtue of its mixed nature, it provides a classic example of the meeting of narrative traditions, the supplanting of older ways by newer. The episodic, pseudofactual mode, even as a local illusion, gives way to the coherence of the action, a fusion seen previously only in drama and the epic and not to appear again, at least in any well-known example, until Richardson and Fielding create their "new species." It is precisely the heterogeneity of *Roxana*, its rebellion against one tradition and movement toward another, that defines Defoe's place, given his earlier works, in the history of prose narrative. One is forced to see his development and grant that he cannot be shaved and pared to fit a single tradition. Once Defoe's concluding instability begins, the ordinary randomness of most of his narratives is left behind, and one begins to see at work, behind Roxana, the motivating consciousness of what Wayne Booth calls an "implied author."[9] Roxana fades from memory, after the somewhat abrupt termination of her story, leaving the impression, not of some naive diarist recounting her own life, not even of wonders selected and epitomized, but of a character subjected to the demanding exigencies of a compelling story. The imaginative power of *Roxana* is almost the opposite of the *Journal*'s. The novel celebrates the manipulation of character, the pyrotechnic display of skillful technique—including the artful reordering of "clock time"—and extends the obvious and unashamed invitation to think of the story as "just" a story, an invitation that can be offered just as blatantly by a new kind of structure as by Fieldingesque commentary. Defoe finally discovers, that is, how he can effectively convey the experience of human isolation, not necessarily by writing a book that is itself a mimesis of disorder and discontinuity, but by structuring the career of his heroine so that its tragic implications are not merely *possible* judgments a reader could make but *necessary* inferences he must draw to experience the book at all. Whether the shift in intention involved vision, or rhetoric, or just formal tinkering, Defoe's final experiment conveys most clearly his profoundest convictions.

Although I am primarily interested in Defoe's experiment for what it tells about the poetics of the novel, it will be necessary to look more closely at the details of Defoe's activity. Roxana and her "new Spouse" have returned to Holland where they are blessed with "a very regular contemplative Life." Still, her past continues to torment her mind. She looks back "on former things with Detestation, and with the utmost Affliction." Not even the "Affluence of a plentiful Fortune . . . not all the things we call Pleasure" can comfort her. She dreams "continually of the most frightful and terrible things imaginable . . . Devils and Monsters; falling into Gulphs . . . *and the like*" (p. 264). What is curious here is that, although Roxana has been a paid mistress, having engaged in some practices with her "old lewd Favorite" which she now views with abhorrence, her psychological hell seems vastly incommensurate with her transgressions. Perhaps Defoe may as yet be unsure about the precise nature of the instability he aims to establish, develop, and resolve, since Roxana tells us that she "languish'd near two Years" in this condition and that "if Providence had not reliev'd" her, she "shou'd have died in little time: *But of that hereafter*" (p. 265), a promise never kept, because Roxana ends doomed, not relieved.[10] She then goes "back to another Scene" to "join it to this End" of her story; the end of the story has been reached sixty-five pages, in this edition, before the end of the plot. For the first and last time in Defoe, a chronological shift signals that the bare materials of story are to take on an affective power. After the shift, Roxana relates the "danger of being known" by her daughter Susan. This situation Defoe develops into a tragic instability leading necessarily to Susan's death and Roxana's moral doom. The progression soon becomes clear: as in dramatic tragedy, formal preparation begins to elicit judgments of probable outcome, intuitive assessments of Roxana's continuing dilemma.

A number of explanatory models for this plot form have been developed. On a rather high level of generality would be Todorov's definition of the " 'ideal' narrative," which "begins with a stable situation which is disturbed by some power or force. There results a state of disequilibrium; by the action of a force directed in the opposite direction, the equilibrium is reestablished; the second equilibrium is similar to the first, but the two are never identical." As useful as this formulation is, it would not make possible a specification of the effect such a story would have on a reader. It is merely a description of the materials of plot and does not suggest an affective, working power. Sacks's definition of the novelistic action is more useful in the present instance: "characters about whose fates we are made to care are introduced in unstable relationships which are then further complicated until the complications are finally resolved by the complete removal of the represented instability." With the addition of the nonformal consideration, "made to care," this is closer to an affective power. But caring is only a precondition of affective response, so even here this is far from *Roxana*. One can care about characters who are fated to be happy, like Lizzy Bennet; and many readers care about Moll. So, as a further specification, there is Sacks's "variant form" of the action: "works in which . . . the characters with whose fates we are most concerned, frequently those whom we are made most to admire, are doomed almost from the outset and make choice after choice which leads to their inevitable misery as well as to the unhappiness of all those related to them positively."[11]

With this model, and the response of "pity and fear" it implies, one can understand just how different from most of Defoe the concluding instability of *Roxana* is. No longer are characters free to wander into and out of the book—some must remain to enact their necessary roles. To accomplish the full revelation of Roxana's downward plunge to damnation, Defoe needs characters with certain specified traits: a Dutch merchant, an Amy, and a Susan. They must reveal certain things about themselves and participate in operations of alignment and opposition. Out of such a concatenation results a narrative power and probability unlike anything else in Defoe. One has stepped out of a false "true story" into a novel, a modification that shifts the entire basis on which individual elements of the story are made to function. For example, the character of a Moll Flanders is of interest per se. No matter what she does, Defoe intends just to create an impression of complex personality. He does not subordinate her personality to a movement toward a fate of some kind. Since the reader cannot discern a probable fate for Moll, she and her actions remain ambiguous. As in Boswell's *London Journal*, the most trivial events are of interest in delineating the ubiquitous ego. In the concluding episode of *Roxana*, revelation of the vivid but static "I" yields to progression. Defoe has an implied standard of both inclusion and exclusion.

Before the shift in chronology, episodic linkage is haphazard and seemingly adventitious: "But in the middle of all this Felicity, a dreadful Disaster befel me, which entirely unhing'd all my Affairs, and threw me back into the same state of Life that I was in before" (p. 51). This disaster, unlike the one that dooms Roxana, just happens. Development for most of the book, as for *Moll*, consists of continuous and variable exposure, not movement *toward* anything one can recognize—other than the end of the book. But by the time the instability has been resolved, the reader has been guided through not only a completed change in character, but the virtual destruction of a personality. No matter what Roxana does, her fate is fixed by her character, which caused the train of events culminating in her complicity in her daughter's death. While Roxana's obduracy brings about her tragic fate, it is her humanity that makes that fate tragic, even if full admiration for her is impossible.

In outline form, Roxana's potentially tragic predicament is that, having finally achieved economic and marital success, she finds her position jeopardized by Susan, a child of her first marriage and one of the many children she has left behind in her march to prosperity. Roxana wants to make up for her past neglect. As Novak points out, while indifferent to her illegitimate children, she has real affection for the offspring of her first marriage.[12] In assisting the girl, Roxana discovers that Susan had been a cook maid in an earlier, debauched household in Pall Mall. Susan knows too much about Roxana's shady past, and is determined to the point of obsession to find her mother, whom she more and more believes to be the now respectable Roxana. Roxana's fears of having her past revealed to her respectable husband force her to what seems, in this summary description, a horrible overreaction: she finds herself virtually agreeing to the murder of her own daughter.

What could conceivably give such a bizarre sequence any tragic power? It is precisely in the lengths to which Defoe went to tie Roxana's character to the events that the special quality of the episode emerges. It is as if Defoe, as implied author, decided to do what he had usually resisted as destructive of the illusion of verisimilitude— give narrative "reasons" for seemingly inexplicable acts. Susan, for example, is not just a mechanical angel of vengeance. She is a carefully designed and plausible threat. It is puzzling, at first, that Roxana does not yield to her yearning to reveal herself to Susan, does not solicit the secrecy that would protect her position. But the danger Susan poses is so palpable, precisely because of the kind of person *she* is. Personality has become determinant. Susan has specific knowledge of Roxana's past. Even more threatening, Susan misunderstands the nature and probable reception (by Roxana's Dutch merchant husband) of that information. Susan knows about the "gallant" company "her Lady had always had in the House; how they us'd to sit up all-Night in the House, gaming and dancing . . . what a vast deal of Money the upper Servants got" (p. 285). But to such a poor orphan, all this elegance just proved what an "Angel" her "Lady" was (p. 290). Even after the Quaker upbraids her for suggesting that the wife of the Dutch merchant, now a noblewoman, could be none other than one who "kept little less than a Gaming-Ordinary," Susan still can see nothing amiss in her admiration.

But Susan's loose tongue would not lead necessarily to tragic consequences if she did not possess a determination often bordering on mania. There is little evidence to support Novak's view that Susan pursues Roxana to gain "money or power."[13] She simply wants to find her mother: "The Girl, a passionate Wench," Amy reports, "knew the worst of it, she cou'd go to Service again, and if she wou'd not own her own Child, she must do as she pleas'd; then she fell into a Passion . . . as if she wou'd kill herself" (pp. 268–269). Not only is Susan "obstinately bent upon the Search" for Roxana (p. 274), she also demonstrates what is to Roxana a frightening resourcefulness, an ability not only to search but ultimately to find: " . . . she was sure, if *Amy* wa'n't, my Lady *Roxana* was, her Mother; and that she wou'd go find her out; *adding*, that she made no doubt but she cou'd do it, for she knew where to enquire the Name of her new Husband" (p. 272). There is no uncertainty here. Roxana's fears are fully justified, as they must be for her fleeing from her daughter to be plausible. Susan's threatening to find Roxana through her husband shows how clearly Defoe sees this part of his task, for Roxana's fears and subsequent actions are inexplicable otherwise. His traits and behavior, past and present, are consistently contrasted to Roxana's, so as to make it clear that he would despise Roxana if he found out about her past transgressions. When Roxana originally rejected his proposal of marriage, he saw the refusal as evidence that she was hiding something, even while she vehemently denied acting on anything but principle. The reader, and Roxana, can imagine how he would respond if he discovered what kind of life she had gone on to live with her "old lewd Favorite" and her other paramours, instead of honorably marrying an honorable man. To complicate matters, he is personally moral and responsible, especially in regard to his own children. Here the opposition to Roxana functions clearly to restrict her possibilities of self-revelation: " . . . he was unwilling any thing that was to call him Father, shou'd upbraid him with leaving him in the World, to be call'd Bastard . . . he was astonish'd to think how I could satisfie myself to be so cruel to an innocent Infant, not yet born" (p. 158). This and other such comments make Roxana's fears seem justified. Whether Defoe somehow knows how his story will end yet or not, he reminds the reader again of the merchant's simple but admirable humanity: "having met with some great Losses and Misfortunes" he "had been in *Holland*" and had "carried his Children" with him (p. 231). In the same kind of exigency Roxana so often found herself, he did not leave his children scattered and helpless orphans. An additional comparison is illuminating. For Moll, the threats of the past are always avoidable. She leaves children scattered all over the place but never suffers for it; indeed, she walks back into her son's life and he welcomes her. For Roxana, the past bequeaths unexpected disaster. Transgressions lead necessarily to retribution.

At earlier points in the novel, before the instability is established, these details of personage and past seem part of Defoe's usual additive, coordinating method, interesting but irrelevant to any probable pattern. Once the instability begins, much later, they are reintegrated with startling force.[14] Roxana cannot reveal herself to this kind of a husband, especially given the marriage laws of the society. She had long ago recognized that women might marry and "very often" find "Trouble . . . taken off of their Hands," but just as often, "so was their Money too" (p. 153). Even earlier Roxana had said, ". . . if I shou'd be a Wife, all I had then, was given up to the Husband, and I was thenceforth to be under his Authority only" (p. 144). Moll too is limited by the dictates of her society and her environment; but one must await the outcome of any episode to see precisely *how*. In *Roxana* social conventions contribute, as fully subordinated elements of thought, specific predictive knowledge about the nature of a character's limited choices and probable fate. As Roxana says: upon concealing her past "depended the whole of my Prosperity" (p. 277).

Something must be said about Amy, for without her Defoe could not have solved some of the problems this new kind of work presented him. One is a matter of plausibility. However serious a threat Susan becomes, Roxana's murdering her own daughter would be hard to accept. The second function of Amy results then from Defoe's choice of point of view. The murder, just as in *Macbeth*, must be done by an agent for the reader to retain even minimal sympathy for Roxana's plight. Nevertheless, Roxana must be complicit, and Defoe establishes her guilt with great skill in a series of scenes. Once the instability begins, one can see technique—the order of representation and the use of purposeful juxtaposition—becoming much more important than in other Defoe narratives. Initially, at Amy's suggestion that "it wou'd be absolutely necessary to murther" Susan, Roxana is "fill'd . . . with Horror" (p. 270). Again one questions, Why does Roxana fail to dismiss Amy, or have her arrested? The question only arises in analysis, since Defoe has so carefully established Amy virtually as Roxana's alter ego. As Roxana says, "to have fall'n upon *Amy*, had been to have murther'd myself" (p. 302). Roxana has put Amy to bed with her own lover and watched the proceedings; Amy has had a child by the Prince's servant at the same time Roxana had hers by the Prince; Amy's economic and social status have risen with Roxana's; and Roxana, after the first suggestion of murder, forgives her, since "it was all of it the Effect of her Excess of Affection and Fidelity to me" (p. 271).

At the next suggestion, Roxana pleads, "do not talk thus, I can't bear it" (p. 273). But soon after, fearing that the Dutch merchant is too close to the real facts, she goes so far as to wish Susan "in Heaven" (p. 284). She then utters prophetically that she "resolv'd" she and the girl would never live "to come to *Holland* together" (p. 291). "Not for killing the Girl yet" (p. 298), still she would have "shed but very few Tears" if Susan had died by "any ordinary Distemper" (p. 302). Part of Defoe's accomplishment here is to balance the reader's attraction and repulsion, to play off the horrible pain Roxana feels at the thought of murder against the almost pathological dread of exposure, with the result a clear tendency toward Roxana's giving in to Amy's devilish proposal, even if only in her mind. The past entails not only disaster but the impossibility of hope: "But there was no help for me in it; all I had to satisfie myself was, that it was my Business to be what I was, and conceal what I had been; that all the Satisfaction I could make him, was to live virtuously for the Time to come, not being able to retrieve what had been in Time past; and this I resolv'd upon, tho' . . . afterwards, I had reason to question my Stability" (p. 301). Her security, however, rests on the futile hope of avoiding her daughter, who would destroy her "Stability" by revealing a past "black as Hell" for which the honest merchant "must have abhor'd" Roxana (p. 301).

Finally, only the naked threat of imminent exposure brings Roxana to something like an acceptance of her own daughter's murder. Satisfied that the Dutch Merchant was still in the dark, having avoided the danger of an extended voyage with Susan aboard by feigning pregnancy, Roxana "began to be pretty easy." But, "in the most unaccountable Manner imaginable," she is "brought to the Point of Destruction." Susan's "Captain" acquaintance remarks casually to Roxana's husband, "I hear your Lady has got a Daughter more than she expected" (p. 296). True, the Dutch Merchant "very happily" for Roxana "took it" that the Captain was referring to Roxana's being with child. But this is too close for comfort. In characteristic—of *this* sequence—and skillful juxtaposition, Defoe has Roxana run to Amy, her counselor, lamenting, "we are all utterly undone"—again explicitly tying the maid's fate to her own (p. 297). Only now does Roxana admit, "I was not for killing the Girl yet." This continual repetition of threat followed by anxiety assimilates *Roxana* to that special class of tragedy which numbers among its members *Macbeth* and *Crime and Punishment*. [15]

Defoe, to be sure, is still feeling his way, even here, but in ways that reveal much about his task. Should he have Roxana recite details of the murder, or leave it mysterious? After reporting Amy's foul deed, Roxana declares that she *"may in time relate more particularly"* the circumstances of the girl's death (p. 303). She does not, except in her disordered dreams, envision the circumstances and here Defoe seems to have made the correct decision. Roxana's fate is to have acquiesced, in order to secure her position, in the death of her daughter. The hellish moral abyss which Roxana recounted before she went "back" has been explained and it is now obvious that she will never escape her "Apparitions." The uncertainty about the girl's death makes all the more terrible the load of guilt Roxana assumed by accepting Amy back. When Roxana does not receive "full Satisfaction" of Amy's innocence (p. 329) and nevertheless welcomes her return, they are joined forever in damnation: Todorov's "equilibrium" has been reestablished, at an awful price.

That the conclusion of *Roxana* seems to be a tragic pattern does not solve another problem: Roxana's character. How is it possible to call her tragic? She is, quite obviously, seriously limited by a single-minded acquisitiveness that seems to bar her, irrevocably, from nobility. Readers may, indeed, admire her ruthlessness, in a way that they do not admire, say, Macbeth's. The comparison, however, is illustrative in another direction. While Macbeth commits objectively greater villainies than Roxana, his "nature," as Lady Macbeth and others attest, is composed of "kindness." In addition, the agonies he experiences upon becoming, in the eyes of his society, a "dead butcher," force one to recognize his humanity and permit a degree of pity for him. Roxana does not have such kindness, at least not until it is too late to have much effect on the reader's opinion of her. Defoe could, perhaps, have solved the problem by showing much earlier a softer side of Roxana. But such a decision would have made Roxana's determination to hide herself from her daughter less plausible, not to mention her complicity in Susan's death. Roxana's obduracy is necessary for the tragedy to take place. Defoe did, however, recognize the problem and tried, perhaps vainly, to deal with it. First, as Jane Jack notes, he shows that "Roxana comes to comprehend the darkness of evil and realizes that she is for ever excluded from the innocent world of the Quaker widow."[16] This, the equivalent of a tragic recognition, is the horror of the guilty soul who will have "ever before" her eyes "the poor Girl herself," her dead daughter (p. 325). Defoe depends, that is, on what is perhaps everyone's natural tendency to feel pity even for deserved misfortune if the suffering that follows is profound enough. Secondly, in what should seem digressive but does not, Roxana tells immediately before the end of the book of her covert efforts to assist her "other Daughter" (p. 328), whom she even takes the dangerous risk of seeing. This meeting "work'd upon" Roxana's "Affections" so much that she had an "infinite Struggle" before she "master'd a strong Inclination" to "discover" herself to her (p. 329). The scene serves to lend some ·necessary humanity to Roxana at a crucial point in her decline, but it may be too little too late. It will remain for later writers to endow characters with tragic stature and the proper balance of noble traits and potential flaws necessary to move readers with a dolorous fate. Even so, Roxana possesses more grandeur, even in her ruthlessness, than the merely pathetic heroes of eighteenth-century "weeping" tragedy, like George Barnwell.

Structural Demands: The Conclusion of "Roxana"

Out of this carefully wrought synthesis of character and morally determined action, qualified and given seriousness by aspects of a represented society, came a new narrative teleology. *Roxana* is not, if I am correct, *one* novel; it is not even one use of narrative. It begins in the older episodic mode of the epitome and shifts to what, in the hands of Richardson and Fielding, was to lead finally to fully realized, continuous instabilities, although only *Clarissa*, a coherent tragic action, develops in well-known eighteenth-century fiction the specific potentialities of *Roxana*. Once the instability in *Roxana* begins, there is a perceptible shift in the very basis of narrative experience; judgments, of probability or significance, are now under the control of an authorial guiding hand. Defoe's new intuition of novelistic form has finally overruled his old episodic habits.

It can now be explained why the ending of *Roxana*, alone among endings of Defoe's narratives, is the only one to have aroused any controversy over its formal appropriateness or adequacy. One might indeed have been alerted to the innovation of *Roxana* before now by the very existence of a question about its completeness. Expectations not aroused in *Moll Flanders* or *Robinson Crusoe* have been created by the final sequence of *Roxana* and must be operating as one nears the end.[17] The very progressive nature of the concluding instability, the sense in which it induces the reader to see Roxana moving toward a tragic fate, is the source of these expectations. It is part of the mimetic "tidiness" of the action form that it requires the most forceful realization of the promised fate, whether it be comic or tragic. The serious action can even require that a character's fate *not* be clearly one thing or another. As a function of the ongoing probable pattern, one expects that Roxana's guilt will be equivalent to her moral doom, an equation reinforced at important points by her suppressed but powerful maternal feelings for Susan: "I cannot but take Notice here, that notwithstanding there was a secret Horror upon my Mind, and I was ready to sink when I came close to her, to salute her; yet it was a secret inconceivable Pleasure to me when I kiss'd her, to know that I kiss'd my own Child . . . I felt something shoot thro' my Blood; my Heart flutter'd . . . I thought I must have taken her in my Arms, and kiss'd her again a thousand times, whether I wou'd or no" (p. 277). Such simple humanity, present in many of Defoe's stories, now has a clear use: it elevates Roxana above mere villainy as well as justifying the horror she will experience at her complicity in the girl's murder. Indeed, much of the power of this sequence derives from the contrast between Roxana's "secret" feelings of longing and pity and the act that she finally must accept as her own. Granting the vast difference in the qualities of the two works, there is yet this similarity between *Roxana* and *Macbeth*: if the deed be done, the spirit will die.

Defoe has in fact met the requirements for completion in *Roxana*, the objectification of the moral doom. The reader's expectations of doom have been fulfilled. For this reason, the "spurious continuation . . . added in the 1740's" only draws out the financial consequences of Roxana's subsequent exposure, adding nothing to the real issue, the moral effect of her actions.[18] The addition therefore *feels* like a sequel. The moment one can say that, one is in a world of narrative very different from Moll's, whose adventures could always have been lengthened, with minor revisions of the concluding paragraphs, without violating the tenuous coherence of her story.

While Defoe has attained completeness, he has not found an appropriate means of closure, the sense of finality experienced at the end of any strong narrative or dramatic pattern. Two problems, one having to do with the genre of tragedy and the other involved with the specific exigencies of this particular story, interfere with the reader's sense of an ending. In tragedy, narrative or dramatic, that involves a moral decline, one often comes to expect that the moment of recognition will be followed by death. To what extent this is just a conventional expectation or, on the contrary, part of the internal necessity of the plot is difficult to say. Why does only Shakespeare, of all those who use the Lear story, end the spectacle with death? From the conventional standpoint, death for Roxana may have afforded a stronger closural force, but it also would have robbed the sequence of some of its unique ethical power. It is Roxana's fate to *live* with what she has done and has therefore become. Of course, such an ending would have required a shift in the point of view—not an impossibility, but certainly awkward, given Defoe's limited narrational repertoire and the vestigial remains of the intention to deceive with a true story.

The other problem results from Defoe's decision to shift chronology. Immediately before the shift, one hears of Roxana's nightmares, her continuing hallucinatory horrors. In novelistic time, the death of Susan has already occurred and Roxana is at this point actually at the end of her *story*, although the *plot* has yet to work itself out. By the time readers go back to learn the cause of her doom and are taken through so many pages of tightly packed, progressive narration, they may inevitably be left with an attenuated sense of the depth of Roxana's suffering. The effect has been seen before the cause. Defoe is trusting the reader's memory, and Roxana again tells of her anguish. Yet somehow it is not the same as seeing the manifestation of the tragic fate take place at the end. Even so, the final paragraph, if read carefully, is an apt if abrupt summation of Roxana's fate: "Here, after some few Years of flourishing, and outwardly happy Circumstances, I fell into a dreadful Course of Calamities, and Amy also; the very Reverse of our former Good Days; the Blast of Heaven seem'd to follow the Injury done the poor Girl, by us both; and I was brought so low again, that my Repentance seem'd to be only the Consequence of my Misery, as my Misery was of my Crime" (pp. 329–330). Susan is dead; the Fates have overtaken Roxana. The attempt to hide the past has been vain, the murder, "by us both," was, like those committed by Macbeth, a wasted and futile gesture.

Although the conclusion of *Roxana* succeeds as a novelistic sequence, it probably fails as narrative tragedy. Roxana is perhaps too flawed a personality, too near a relative to Moll and Singleton, and without the redeeming virtues of intellect and imagination earlier tragic figures had, to carry off successfully the tragic effect. No doubt the potential ambiguity of first-person narration is another difficulty, although Booth has shown how easily I-narrators can communicate necessary information.[19] But as an experiment in tragic form, it is far more interesting than many of the dramatic tragedies, such as *The Fair Penitent* and *Jane Shore*, that held the boards when *Roxana* appeared. Indeed, Defoe's last major narrative is the first important example of how tragedy not only shifted to narrative but descended the social scale. The journey was to take nearly two centuries and would end in complex tragic actions by George Eliot, Hardy, Conrad, Hemingway, Faulkner, and many others. French narrative would be similarly enriched, beginning with Prévost's *Manon Lescaut*, a book that as much as *Roxana* stands out as a formal innovation. For reasons too complex to deal with here, the leveling process had already begun that ultimately was to leave writers such as Arthur Miller and Tennessee Williams only the "little" people, like Willy Loman, as fit subjects for tragedy. George Lillo would write his "tradesman's tragedy," *The London Merchant*, in 1731, the year of Defoe's death. No longer would elevated social status, even nobility, be sufficient guarantors that a character's fate would move an audience. Narrative, beginning with the experiment of *Roxana*, reveals an advantage, given the conditions under which tragedy would be written in the next two centuries, over drama: it does not depend, as drama does, on objective tokens of nobility of soul. Rather, the inside of a character is seen, with more economy than is afforded by the soliloquy. First-person narrators, even if they are rogues like Lazarillo, tend to seduce the reader fairly easily to their causes. Finally, then, in *Roxana*, Defoe makes a definite virtue of his narrator's point of view, one originally adopted, with Crusoe, for other reasons entirely. Viewed from the outside, Roxana would not move the reader with her fate—she would be getting what she deserves, perhaps less. Defoe achieves what success he does with his last important narrative because he has finally discovered the virtues of authorial distance and control. Defoe is in no important sense Roxana. He stands back and, with unusual detachment, arranges the details of Roxana's tragedy so that the reader may be affected by it. He does what was then unheard of in narrative and what has now apparently gone out of style: through his artistry he imposes form on created experience and demands that one judge a character. Novelistic potentialities his other works contain. Only the conclusion of *Roxana* realized the formal possibilities that became the traditional English novel.

VI

Defoe and Pressures on the Early Novel

UNDERSTANDING DEFOE'S DEVELOPMENT should allow readers not only to place him, with some descriptive accuracy, within the history of prose fiction, but also to use him to clarify the nature of those various narrative forms that developed after him, particularly in the eighteenth century. His own attempts to employ narrative in divergent fashions serve, when understood in their general significance, as a paradigm for the possibilities of diverse use in narrative itself. In his career are seen the forces and tendencies at work that mold the later history of prose fiction and make possible the triumphs of the traditional novel. Indeed, few writers participate more than Defoe in so many of the general possibilities for prose fiction.

He wrote no single coherent example of a traditional novel. Only the conclusion of *Roxana* shows what it was to become—progressive, probable, predictive. He wrote two important examples of works most critics balk at calling novels: *A Journal of the Plague Year* and the *Memoirs of a Cavalier*. A refusal unequivocally to admit them into the house of the novel is an appropriate response to an intuitive experience of their truthlike structures. Neither presents even ambiguous internal evidence of being a fiction, much less a plotted, traditional novel. They deal, not in the novelistic world of probability, but in the historical world of certainty, even though external information indicates that they are indeed fictions. A third category—both parts of *Robinson Crusoe, Captain Singleton, Moll Flanders, Colonel Jack*, and most of *Roxana*—are neither traditional novels nor opaque imitations of true stories, but what I have called epitomes. Without revealing the strong plot of the traditional novel, they are yet recognizable fictions, and are frequently called novels. None of them, with the exception of *Moll Flanders*, is "pure," in the sense of being, on their own terms, unmixed refinements of the pleasures of personality; they also contain moments that hint at the purposeful teleology of the traditional novel, others that seem to move them toward the historicity of the *Journal* and the *Memoirs*, and even moments that hint at parabolic or satirical use.

Within Defoe, who has seemed to many to be such a naive and uniform author, exist three distinct ways of ordering narrative experience: as illusions, sometimes his stories are historical, at times ambiguously fictional, at others positively fictional in a protonovelistic manner. Stepping back from Defoe for a moment, one sees that these three uses of narrative correspond to a more general paradigm of eighteenth-century narrative. Clearly, a number of narratives are being written that one would not want to call novels even though they are obviously fictional, and they are not all imitations of true stories like the *Journal*. Some, like *Gulliver's Travels*, employ narrative to attack targets external to the created world of the text. Others, like *Rasselas*, use narrative to enforce a clearly specifiable set of precepts. Yet both these works share with the *Journal* a use of narrative for some purpose other than the representation and exploration of personality for its own sake. As a general rule then, at least in the eighteenth century, a narrative fiction is not experienced even ambiguously as a novel unless it meets some minimal criterion of involving the reader in the lives of characters created primarily for their own sakes. The use can be satiric, didactic, pseudohistorical, as in Defoe, or something else; such works will tend to be called novels only if they simultaneously evince an interest in personality.

The term "novel," then, signifies a continuum of possible effects, ranging from the purity of the traditional novel to mixed forms that combine an interest in personality with other, sometimes conflicting, interests. To the extent that the second intention takes over, one's sense of a narrative's belonging to the general class "novel" will be attenuated. At the same time, thoroughly ideological structures, such as *Tristram Shandy* or Camus's *The Plague* and *The Stranger*, can be experienced as novels so long as they manage to induce the reader to care for the characters.

On the other hand is that large body of works I have called the traditional novel. Apart from their strong structures, their progressive and powerful movement toward a qualitatively defined fate for the central character or characters, they exhibit other general features, as functions of their structures, that allow them to be recognized unambiguously as novels. Of course, they represent personality and its permutations for the inherent interest of such representation, and not for some end primarily satiric, ideological, or historical. They deal in probabilities, not certainties. The reader recognizes that he is in a narrative world controlled by the guiding consciousness of an implied author, whose decisions are manifested on every page and dictate local responses to the likely direction of story. Curiously, the eighteenth century displays few totally coherent works of this unmixed type. Richardson and Fielding are the only well-known authors of this entirely new species, although many other writers explore personality in ways that allow readers to experience their works ambiguously as novels.

Two examples will have to suffice here. It is evidence of some sort that, while Smollett's *Humphry Clinker* is usually assumed to be a novel, his first narrative, *Roderick Random*, is usually called some version of the picaresque. The distinction is important, because it indicates readers have felt a difference, just as many students of American literature insist upon distinguishing the novel from the romance. Smollett himself, in his preface, describes his intention: "Of all kinds of satire, there is none so entertaining and universally improving as that which is introduced, as it were occasionally, in the course of an interesting story." The revealing word here is "occasionally." What Smollett describes is his practice of deflecting a story with clearly novelistic potentiality (in the traditional sense) to the ends of attacking specific social and political targets outside the book. As he continues, the "reader gratifies his curiosity in pursuing the adventures of a person in whose favor he is prepossessed; he espouses his cause, he sympathizes with him in distress; his indignation is heated against the authors of his calamity . . . the contrast between dejected virtue and insulting vice appears with greater aggravation; and every impression having a double force on the imagination, the memory retains the circumstance, and the heart improves by the example."[1] Yet the effect Smollett achieved was very different from this combination of pity for a created character (novel) and anger at the viciousness of the real world outside the book (satire). Perhaps readers cannot simultaneously perform both operations, make both judgments. For whatever reason, Roderick remains an unattractive, often brutal, character whose primary function, as in the famous Cartagena episode, is to serve as a device to sustain the satiric attack. The impulse to satirize somehow interferes with the representation of personality as Smollett intended it, just as it prevented Swift from making Gulliver's character consistent. Yet, since Roderick is sufficiently complex and consistent to indicate Smollett's interest lies primarily in his representation, one can experience *Roderick Random* as a novel: picaresque, in that it satirizes, novel, in that it explores personality. Nevertheless, the book is divided, no matter how ingeniously critics meld its two informing principles.

Roderick Random was Smollett's first novel. My second example of a narrative with a split principle of being is Goldsmith's only "novel," what Byron called the "most exquisite of all romance in miniature," *The Vicar of Wakefield*. David Richter has described the way in which Goldsmith wrote the two "halves of The *Vicar . . .* to diverse ends." The first part of the novel, up to the end of chapter seventeen, is "a morally serious comedy of a kind with which readers of Fielding are familiar." But after the narrator, Dr. Primrose, sets out to "reclaim a lost child to virtue," the "novel accordingly turns into an apologue testifying to the power of faith to remain steadfast in a world replete with evils."[2] If Richter is correct, then Goldsmith, as well as Smollett, was reacting to some of the same pressures bearing on the gestating novel that I have traced in Defoe. Finding certain fundamental difficulties he could not overcome in his attempt to write what would have been the first serious, first-person, comic action in English literature, Goldsmith switched instead to a nonnovelistic use of narrative, one his friend Johnson had so successfully employed a few years earlier in *Rasselas*. Novel transmutes into parable and, by the end of the book, Goldsmith must decide which expectations he will satisfy.[3]

Many other examples could be given of eighteenth-century narratives that do not adhere to single principles of proceeding, novelistic or otherwise. Indeed, a thorough study of such works is needed. In conclusion, I should like to suggest the source of this tendency to allow narrative to transmute, as it were, in mid-book. The traditional novel, I have argued, celebrates representation for its own sake; yet it was born in a century that insisted literature must have a purpose. All of the uses of narrative that I have called nonnovelistic, in their pure forms—satire, apologue, pseudohistory—are attempts to turn narrative into the service of virtue, or at least information or ideology. The traditional novel, on the other hand, found ways to subordinate ideas to the moving, powerful representation of created personality. As Rader has recently noted, "the cultural demand—enthusiastically accepted by Fielding, Richardson, and Fanny Burney—that novels must be morally pure and efficacious posed a problem in formal accommodation for these novelists that permitted the success of their early novels, stultified their later ones, and found a beautiful solution in the exquisite actions of Jane Austen."[4] Yet it was not just ideology that impinged on the new territory of the novel, as Defoe teaches, but any use that would draw narrative away from its mimetic function. If Defoe found no completely satisfactory way to escape from the determinate and impersonal world of history, and from the burdens of didacticism or social commentary, and declined to venture boldly into the self-justifying realm of the novel, his attempts to free himself from the constraints of older uses of narrative tell a story that points unmistakably toward similar difficulties that later fabulators will have.

Notes

CHAPTER I
Defoe and Narrative Traditions

1. Samuel Johnson, *The Rambler*, 3:20.
2. See my "Defoe's Political Rhetoric and the Problem of Irony."
3. Ralph W. Rader's theory that all of Defoe's first-person stories are imitations of true narratives, and therefore clearly not traditional novels, is a powerful explanation of many features of Defoe's texts. My attempt to qualify his findings should not obscure my debt to his thought. See, for example, "Defoe, Richardson, Joyce, and the Concept of Form in the Novel." The Stephen quotation is from "Defoe's Novels," 1:31.
4. Alan D. McKillop, *The Early Masters of English Fiction*, p. 25.
5. David Goldknopf, *The Life of the Novel*, p. 52.
6. Ian Watt, *The Rise of the Novel*, p. 96.
7. Everett Zimmerman, *Defoe and the Novel*, p. 17.
8. McKillop, *Masters*, p. 16.
9. See Robert Scholes and Robert Kellogg, *The Nature of Narrative*.
10. See Wolfgang Iser, "The Current Situation of Literary Theory: Key Concepts and the Imaginary."
11. Daniel Defoe, *Moll Flanders*, p. 2. Subsequent references are in the text.
12. J. Paul Hunter, *The Reluctant Pilgrim*, p. 19.
13. Morse Peckham has opposed "situational interpretation," in which a work yields insights to a "theoretically finite" number of approaches, to "emergent interpretation," in which "any literary text (or any nonliterary text, for that

matter) can be used to exemplify any explanation" ("The Infinitude of Pluralism," p. 810).

14. Maximillian E. Novak, *Defoe and the Nature of Man*, p. 3; G. A. Starr, *Defoe and Spiritual Autobiography*, p. xi; Watt, *Rise*, p. 117; E. M. W. Tillyard, *The Epic Strain in the English Novel*, p. 45; Edwin B. Benjamin, "Symbolic Elements in *Robinson Crusoe*," p. 210.

15. John J. Richetti, *Defoe's Narratives*, p. 7.

16. "Daniel De Foe," in Pat Rogers, ed., *Defoe: The Critical Heritage*, p. 154.

17. Walter Wilson, *Memoirs of the Life and Times of Daniel Defoe*, 3:443; anonymous review, in Rogers, *Heritage*, p. 135.

18. Watt, *Rise*, p. 74.

19. Arthur Wellesley Secord, *Studies in the Narrative Method of Defoe*, p. 233.

20. John Stuart Mill, *On Liberty*, p. 42.

21. Scholes and Kellogg, *Nature of Narrative*, p. 191.

22. Virginia Woolf, "How It Strikes a Contemporary," p. 244; Wayne C. Booth, *The Rhetoric of Fiction*, esp. pp. 137–147.

23. Hunter, *Reluctant Pilgrim*, p. 14.

24. Watt, *Rise*, p. 67.

25. See n. 10.

26. Martin Price, *To the Palace of Wisdom*, p. 264.

27. *Defoe's Review*, ed. Arthur W. Secord, 1:82; *The Political History of the Devil*, p. 370.

28. McKillop, *Masters*, p. 8.

29. Rader, "Defoe, Richardson, Joyce," p. 42. What does one do when external sources indicate that a narrative is a fabrication, but internal form demands that the narrative be viewed as true? I attempt an answer in the third chapter.

30. Ralph W. Rader, "The Literary Theoretical Contribution of Sheldon Sacks."

31. Sheldon Sacks, *Fiction and the Shape of Belief*, p. 15. Sacks's book has recently come under close scrutiny. See Rader's discussion, mentioned above, and the other contributions on Sacks's work in *Critical Inquiry* 6.

32. Victor Shklovsky, quoted in Tzvetan Todorov, *The Poetics of Prose*, p. 21.

33. Daniel Defoe, *A Journal of the Plague Year*, p. 33. Subsequent references are in the text.

34. Daniel Defoe, *Roxana*, pp. 270–271. Further references appear in the text.

35. Murray Krieger, "Fiction and Historical Reality: The Hourglass and the Sands of Time," p. 55.

CHAPTER 11
"*Robinson Crusoe*"

1. Henry James, Preface to *The Tragic Muse*, p. 81.
2. See Quentin Kraft, "*Robinson Crusoe* and the Story of the Novel."
3. See, for example, Todorov, *The Poetics of Prose*.
4. Starr, *Spiritual Autobiography*, p. 72; McKillop, *Masters*, p. 21; Watt, *Rise*, Chapter 3.
5. Frank Ellis, Introduction to *Twentieth-Century Views of Robinson Crusoe*, p. 1.
6. R. S. Crane, *The Languages of Criticism and the Structure of Poetry*, esp. pp. 3–38. For the fullest treatment of the implications of critical pluralism, see Wayne C. Booth, *Critical Understanding: The Powers and Limits of Pluralism*. For Kermode, see *The Genesis of Secrecy*, esp. pp. 1–21.
7. Todorov's "undertaking" is based on Valéry's remark, "Literature is, and cannot be anything but, a kind of extension and application of certain properties of language" (*Poetics of Prose*, p. 19). For my purposes, it will be useful to consider narrative as just another choice, among many, that authors make to solve the particular problems their own brands of creation present. Defoe, of course, does not initially "choose" narrative—the pseudofactual mode demands it, just as it does I-narration—but he and later writers discover through experimentation its inherent strengths and liabilities for portraying inner states of being.
8. Crane, *Languages*, pp. 182–183.
9. See David H. Richter, *Fable's End*, pp. 171–176.
10. Paul Alkon argues that "the final shape of memories induced by a text would have to be accepted as one of its formal attributes" (*Defoe and Fictional Time*, p. 11). While responses to a text cannot really be said to be a part of the text itself, it is true that one must boldly commit the affective fallacy to understand Defoe's forms.
11. *National Review*, in Rogers, *Critical Heritage*, p. 129.
12. John Bayley, "Character and Consciousness," pp. 225–226.
13. See Wolfgang Iser, *The Implied Reader*.
14. Daniel Defoe, *Robinson Crusoe*, p. 1. Subsequent references are in the text.
15. See Chapter 1, n. 2.
16. See John Robert Moore, *Daniel Defoe: Citizen of the Modern World*, p. 25.
17. McKillop, *Masters*, p. 10.
18. Sacks, *Fiction and the Shape of Belief*, pp. 22–24.
19. See R. S. Crane, "The Concept of Plot and the Plot of *Tom Jones*," esp. pp. 637–638; and Sacks, *Fiction and the Shape of Belief*, p. 107.

20. See Chapter 1, n. 3.

21. Reported by Graves, in *The Prose Works of William Wordsworth*, 3:468.

22. Jean-Jacques Rousseau, *Émile*, p. 211.

23. James Sutherland, *Defoe*, pp. 245, 234.

24. I have benefited from two studies of early French narrative: Philip Stewart, *Imitation and Illusion in the French Memoir-Novel, 1700–1750*, and English Showalter, Jr., *The Evolution of the French Novel, 1641–1782*.

25. [Gatien de Courtilz], *The Memoirs of the Count de Rocheforte*, p. 118.

26. The change is the reverse of what transpires in the *Lazarillo*.

27. For Courtilz and Defoe, see Wilhelm Füger, "Courtilz de Sandras, der französische Defoe."

28. See Kraft, "*Robinson Crusoe*."

29. Leo Braudy, "Daniel Defoe and the Anxieties of Autobiography," p. 82; Charles Gildon, *The Life and Strange Surprizing Adventures of Mr. D . . . . . De F . .*, *of London, Hosier*, in Rogers, *Critical Heritage*, p. 45.

30. Watt, *Rise*, p. 65.

31. Samuel Johnson, *Johnson on Shakespeare*, 8:704.

32. *National Review*, in Rogers, *Critical Heritage*, p. 129.

33. Zimmerman, *Defoe and the Novel*, p. 29, n. 7.

34. Ibid., pp. 28–29.

35. Kraft, "*Robinson Crusoe*," p. 538; Stanley E. Fish, *Surprised by Sin*.

36. For the application of Sir Karl Popper's theory of unintended consequences to literary studies, see Ralph W. Rader, "Fact, Theory, and Literary Explanation," pp. 250–253.

37. For the implied author, see Wayne C. Booth, *The Rhetoric of Fiction*, pp. 71–73.

38. Tillyard, *Epic Strain*, p. 39.

39. See Stewart, *Imitation and Illusion*, pp. 22–32.

40. Sir Philip Sidney, *A Defence of Poetry*, p. 52; Dominique Bouhours, *The Art of Criticism*, p. 197.

41. Stewart, *Imitation and Illusion*, p. 25.

42. Maximillian E. Novak, "Defoe's Theory of Fiction," p. 660.

43. Daniel Defoe, *Colonel Jack*, p. 1. Further references are in the text.

44. Watson Nicholson, *The Historical Sources of Defoe's Journal of the Plague Year*. Nicholson is largely ignored today because he commits an interesting non sequitur: because the *Journal's* intrinsic form is historical, the book is a veritable history.

45. G. A. Starr, *Defoe and Casuistry*, p. 201.

46. Wilson, *Memoirs*, 3:442; De Quincey, in Rogers, *Critical Heritage*, p. 118.

47. Martin C. Battestin, "Fielding," p. 77.

Notes

CHAPTER III
The Impersonal Narrator

1. Daniel Defoe, *The Farther Adventures of Robinson Crusoe*, t.p. Subsequent references, in the text, are to *Romances and Narratives*, vol. 2.

2. Gildon, *Life*, in Rogers, *Critical Heritage*, p. 46.

3. Paul Dottin, *The Life and Strange Surprizing Adventures of Daniel Defoe*, p. 203.

4. Defoe, *Farther Adventures*, 2:vii; Gildon, *Life*, in Rogers, *Critical Heritage*, p. 47.

5. Gildon, *Life*, in Rogers, *Critical Heritage*, p. 42.

6. Ibid., pp. 41, 46, 44.

7. James T. Boulton, Introduction to *Memoirs of a Cavalier*, p. xi. Subsequent references to the *Memoirs* from this edition are in the text. John Robert Moore, *A Checklist of the Writings of Daniel Defoe*, pp. 175–176; Malcolm J. Bosse, *Introduction to Memoirs of a Cavalier*, p. 8.

8. Thomas De Quincey, "Homer and the Homeridae," 6:84–85.

9. See R. S. Crane, "Ernest Hemingway: 'The Killers.' "

10. John R. Searle, "The Logical Status of Fictional Discourse," p. 325.

11. See Ralph W. Rader, "Literary Form in Factual Narrative: The Example of Boswell's *Johnson*."

12. Secord, *Studies*, p. 208; Dottin, *Life*, p. 213; Novak, *Defoe and the Nature of Man*, pp. 141–142; William P. Trent, *Daniel Defoe: How to Know Him*, p. 213; Moore, *Daniel Defoe*, p. 260; Boulton, Introduction to *Memoirs*, p. xii; Zimmerman, *Defoe and the Novel*, p. 150.

13. Boulton, Introduction to *Memoirs*, p. xii.

14. Zimmerman, *Defoe and the Novel*, p. 191.

15. Richetti, *Defoe's Narratives*, p. 7.

16. Defoe, *Review*, 7:344.

17. Ibid., 6:233.

18. Ibid., 1:149, 3:170–171.

19. Moore, *Daniel Defoe*, p. 262.

20. W. Austin Flanders, "Defoe's *Journal of the Plague Year* and the Modern Urban Experience," in Max Byrd, ed., *Daniel Defoe: A Collection of Critical Essays*, p. 151.

21. Johnson, *Johnson on Shakespeare*, 7:65.

22. See Manuel Schonhorn, "Defoe's *Journal of the Plague Year*: Topography and Intention."

23. Sutherland, *Defoe*, p. 241; Louis Landa, Introduction to *A Journal of the Plague Year*, p. xxxiv.

24. Starr, *Defoe and Casuistry*, p. 58; Zimmerman, *Defoe and the Novel*, p. 110.
25. Starr, *Defoe and Casuistry*, p. 59; Zimmerman, *Defoe and the Novel*, p. 110.
26. Zimmerman, *Defoe and the Novel*, p. 108.
27. Ibid., p. 119.
28. Virginia Woolf, "Robinson Crusoe," p. 45.
29. Joseph Addison, *Spectator* no. 412.
30. Sophocles, *Oedipus Rex*, 2.18.
31. Johnson, *Rambler*, 3:318–319.
32. Starr, *Defoe and Casuistry*, p. 56.
33. For this reason, Kermode finds the analysis of narrative in terms of common experience, what he calls "carnal" interpretation, relatively unexciting, preferring instead the uniqueness of "spiritual" interpretation, in which the critic, as seer, ferrets out (creates?) the text's recondite meaning.
34. For a reading that assimilates the two books, see James E. Rocks, "Camus Reads Defoe: *A Journal of the Plague Year* as a Source of *The Plague*."
35. William Nelson, *Fact or Fiction: The Dilemma of the Renaissance Storyteller*, p. 110.
36. Henry James, "The Art of Fiction," pp. 30–31.
37. Occasionally, a naive novelist will come along and assume that his task is still to create a strong, value-charged, fictional system; for an analysis of the difficulties such an author might encounter in the modern age, see my "*One Flew Over the Cuckoo's Nest*: Rhetoric and Vision."

CHAPTER IV
The Captain and Moll

1. Samuel Johnson, Preface to *A Dictionary of the English Language*, p. 245; Todorov, *Poetics of Prose*, p. 93.
2. Todorov, *Poetics of Prose*, p. 95.
3. Jacques Barzun, *Clio and the Doctors*, p. 93.
4. Todorov, *Poetics of Prose*, p. 95.
5. Daniel Defoe, *Captain Singleton*, p. 1. Subsequent references appear in the text.
6. For example, compare Bob's views to what Defoe says in the *Review*, 4:186, 256, 299.
7. Roland Barthes, *A Lover's Discourse*, pp. 6–7.
8. Alain Robbe-Grillet, "A Future for the Novel," p. 22.
9. Barthes, *Discourse*, p. 23.
10. Rader, "Defoe, Richardson, Joyce," pp. 42, 44–45.

11. Robbe-Grillet, "Future," p. 22 (my emphasis); see Maximillian E. Novak, "Defoe's 'Indifferent Monitor': The Complexity of Moll Flanders."

12. Watt, *Rise*, p. 130.

13. See H. L. Koonce, "Moll's Muddle: Defoe's Use of Irony in *Moll Flanders*."

14. Watt is one among many to assume that Defoe tried to create a traditional novel and failed: Defoe's "moral attitude to his creation is as shallow and devious and easily deflected as his heroine's" (*Rise*, p. 125).

15. Virginia Woolf, "Defoe," p. 92.

16. See Paul Fussell, *The Great War and Modern Memory*.

17. Stewart, *Imitation and Illusion*, p. 27.

18. Johnson, *Rambler*, 3:22, 24.

19. *Moll Flanders*, pp. 402–403.

20. Novak, *Defoe and the Nature of Man*, p. 161.

21. Ibid., p. 81.

22. Ibid., p. 129.

23. Sacks, *Fiction and the Shape of Belief*, esp. Chapters 1 and 4.

24. For Fielding, see Martin C. Battestin, *The Moral Basis of Fielding's Art*. For an argument against the "soft" interpretation of the Fourth Voyage, see Rader, "Fact, Theory, and Literary Explanation," pp. 255–258.

25. *Review*, 1:294; Novak, *Defoe and the Nature of Man*.

26. Rawdon Wilson, "The Bright Chimera: Character as a Literary Term," p. 729.

CHAPTER V

Novelistic Possibilities

1. Krieger, "Fiction and Historical Reality," pp. 56, 55.

2. Rader, "Defoe, Richardson, Joyce," p. 35.

3. *National Review*, in Rogers, *Critical Heritage*, p. 129.

4. *Colonel Jack*, like *Moll* and the *Journal*, appeared in Defoe's most productive year, 1722.

5. McKillop, *Masters*, p. 37; Bonamy Dobrée, *English Literature in the Early Eighteenth Century*, p. 425; Robert D. Hume, "The Conclusion of Defoe's *Roxana*: Fiasco or Tour de Force?," p. 481; Wallace Jackson, "*Roxana* and the Development of Defoe's Fiction," p. 192.

6. Hume notes Defoe's "unusual deviation from the normal linear time-scheme" ("Conclusion," p. 483), but does not indicate that he perceives Defoe's shift in narrative mode. David Leon Higdon also mentions the shift but does not seem to think it important ("The Critical Fortunes and Misfortunes of Defoe's

Roxana"). Overlooking the shift has led to some serious misreading: Jackson argues that "before the murder of Susan" Roxana "is troubled with fearful dreams" ("*Roxana*," p. 189); Zimmerman cites the "Apparitions" passage as evidence that "even before the murder" Roxana's "inner world" is "bringing her to the point of madness" (*Defoe and the Novel*, p. 171).

7. Many have called Roxana or her story tragic, but the term has usually meant an attitude or particular kind of subject rather than a structure. Jackson, for example, thinks Roxana is tragic because she is sinful, a standard that would make Iago the most tragic of all characters. Hume comes close to my view of the book's conclusion, but he argues too strongly that the tragic pattern is present from the beginning; I cannot see that "we are from the start made aware of the catastrophe toward which Roxana is heading" ("Conclusion," p. 482). Indeed, it is only the existence of a probable, progressive pattern—the achievement of the traditional novel—that allows for such predictive knowledge. Sutherland is more nearly correct when he argues that a happy ending is perfectly possible until "Defoe decided that his story was going to include cold-blooded murder" (*Daniel Defoe*, in Byrd, *Daniel Defoe*, p. 145).

8. Sheldon Sacks, "*Clarissa* and the Tragic Traditions," p. 197.

9. Booth, *Rhetoric of Fiction*, pp. 71–77.

10. Jackson notes that for "neither statement does the novel provide a 'hereafter' " ("*Roxana*," p. 194, n. 30).

11. Todorov, *Poetics of Prose*, p. 111; Sacks, *Fiction and the Shape of Belief*, pp. 15, 21. Obviously, the extent of any reader's admiration for Roxana would influence where the book is placed in the tragic traditions.

12. Maximillian E. Novak, "Crime and Punishment in Defoe's *Roxana*," p. 454.

13. Ibid., p. 455.

14. The concluding instability of *Roxana* did not develop inevitably from what came before. Nothing in the mode of episodic connection, or subject matter, before the conclusion rules out lengthening the string of adventures and finishing up in his ordinary perfunctory manner. Even so, Higdon is partly correct when he argues that "whatever power the last third of the book possesses results from the careful preparation in the first two-thirds" ("Critical Fortunes," p. 69). The exigencies of the final tragic instability do require selective reintegration of many elements. But much that is prepared for, like the reinvolvement of Roxana's first husband, Defoe refrains from bringing up again. While Higdon is perceptive to note that "we can now see the cook as well as the cookery," it is also true that Defoe's recipe for the last part of the book does not require a number of earlier ingredients ("Critical Fortunes," p. 82).

15. Novak observes that Roxana, like Raskolnikov, "has terrible dreams . . . and feels an urge to confess" ("Crime and Punishment," p. 458).

16. Jack, Introduction to *Roxana*, p. xiii.

17. Richter, *Fable's End*, p. 176. The expectations for closure and completeness are so weak in Defoe's other works that seldom does anyone even question whether the endings are appropriate. With Moll, for example, the issue is usually whether her repentance is really permanent, enduring until the conclusion of her story.

18. See Moore, *Checklist*, p. 185.

19. Starr argues that it is first-person narration which makes Roxana's "entire character extremely ambiguous" (*Spiritual Autobiography*, p. 164). This is true, to the extent that, in Defoe's hands, I-narration presented insoluble problems. In absolute terms, later authors have demonstrated that first-person narration can communicate almost anything third-person narration can (see Booth, *Rhetoric of Fiction*, pp. 150–151).

CHAPTER VI
Defoe and Pressures on the Early Novel

1. Tobias Smollett, *Roderick Random*, p. xv.

2. Richter, *Fable's End*, p. 172; Oliver Goldsmith, *The Vicar of Wakefield*, p. 87; Richter, *Fable's End*, p. 174.

3. Richter discusses Goldsmith's problem, *Fable's End*, pp. 174–175.

4. Rader, "The Literary Theoretical Contribution of Sheldon Sacks," p. 189.

Works Cited

Addison, Joseph. *Spectator* no. 412.

Alkon, Paul K. *Defoe and Fictional Time*. Athens, Ga.: University of Georgia Press, 1979.

Barthes, Roland. *A Lover's Discourse*. Translated by Richard Howard. New York: Hill and Wang, 1978.

Barzun, Jacques. *Clio and the Doctors: Psycho-History, Quanto-History, and History*. Chicago: University of Chicago Press, 1974.

Battestin, Martin C. "Fielding." In *The English Novel: Select Bibliographical Guides*. Edited by A. E. Dyson. London: Oxford University Press, 1974.

———. *The Moral Basis of Fielding's Art*. Middletown, Ct.: Wesleyan University Press, 1959.

Bayley, John. "Character and Consciousness." *New Literary History* 5 (1974):225–235.

Benjamin, Edwin B. "Symbolic Elements in *Robinson Crusoe*." *Philological Quarterly* 30 (1951):206–211.

Boardman, Michael M. "Defoe's Political Rhetoric and the Problem of Irony." *Tulane Studies in English* 22 (1977):87–102.

———. "*One Flew Over the Cuckoo's Nest*: Rhetoric and Vision." *The Journal of Narrative Technique* 9 (1979):171–183.

Booth, Wayne C. *Critical Understanding: The Powers and Limits of Pluralism*. Chicago: University of Chicago Press, 1979.

———. *The Rhetoric of Fiction*. Chicago: University of Chicago Press, 1961.

Bosse, Malcolm J. *Introduction to Memoirs of a Cavalier*. New York: Garland, 1972.

Bouhours, Dominique. *The Art of Criticism*. In *The Continental Model*. Edited by Scott Elledge and Donald Schier. 1960. Revised. Ithaca, N.Y.: Cornell University Press, 1970.

Boulton, James T. Introduction to *Memoirs of a Cavalier*. London: Oxford University Press, 1972.

Braudy, Leo. "Daniel Defoe and the Anxieties of Autobiography." *Genre* 6 (1973):76–97.

Byrd, Max, ed. *Daniel Defoe: A Collection of Critical Essays*. Englewood Cliffs, N.J.: Prentice-Hall, 1976.

Crane, R. S. "The Concept of Plot and the Plot of *Tom Jones*." In *Critics and Criticism, Ancient and Modern*. Chicago: University of Chicago Press, 1952.

———. "Ernest Hemingway: 'The Killers.'" In *The Idea of the Humanities and Other Essays*. 2 vols. Chicago: University of Chicago Press, 1967.

———. *The Languages of Criticism and the Structure of Poetry*. Toronto: University of Toronto Press, 1953.

[de Courtilz, Gatien]. *The Memoirs of the Count de Rocheforte*. London: 1696.

De Quincey, Thomas. "Homer and the Homeridae." In *The Collected Writings of Thomas De Quincey*. Edited by David Masson. 14 vols. Edinburgh: A. and C. Black, 1889–90.

Defoe, Daniel. *Captain Singleton*. Edited by Shiv K. Kumar. London: Oxford University Press, 1973.

———. *Colonel Jack*. Edited by Samuel Holt Monk. London: Oxford University Press, 1970.

———. *The Farther Adventures of Robinson Crusoe*. In *Romances and Narratives*. Edited by G. A. Aitken. 16 vols. 1895. Reprint. New York: AMS Press, 1974.

———. *A Journal of the Plague Year*. Edited by Louis Landa. London: Oxford University Press, 1969.

———. *Memoirs of a Cavalier*. Edited by James T. Boulton. London: Oxford University Press, 1972.

———. *Moll Flanders*. Edited by George Starr. London: Oxford University Press, 1971.

———. *The Political History of the Devil*. London, 1726.

———. *Robinson Crusoe*. Edited by J. Donald Crowley. London: Oxford University Press, 1972.

———. *Roxana*. Edited by Jane Jack. London: Oxford University Press, 1969.

Dobrée, Bonamy. *English Literature in the Early Eighteenth Century*. Oxford: Clarendon Press, 1959.

Dottin, Paul. *The Life and Strange Surprizing Adventures of Daniel Defoe*. New York: Macauly, 1929.

Ellis, Frank. Introduction to *Twentieth-Century Views of Robinson Crusoe*. Englewood Cliffs, N.J.: Prentice-Hall, 1969.

• Fish, Stanley E. *Surprised by Sin: The Reader in Paradise Lost*. New York: St. Martin's Press, 1967.

Flanders, W. Austin. "Defoe's *Journal of the Plague Year* and the Modern Urban Experience." *Centennial Review* 16 (1972). Reprinted in *Daniel Defoe: A Collection of Critical Essays*. Edited by Max Byrd. Englewood Cliffs, N.J.: Prentice-Hall, 1976.

Füger, Wilhelm. "Courtilz de Sandras, der französische Defoe." *Die Neueren Sprachen* 9 (1963):407–416.

Fussell, Paul. *The Great War and Modern Memory*. New York: Oxford University Press, 1975.

Gildon, Charles. *The Life and Strange Surprizing Adventures of Mr. D . . . . . De F . ., of London, Hosier*. London, 1719.

Goldknopf, David. *The Life of the Novel*. Chicago: University of Chicago Press, 1972.

Goldsmith, Oliver. *The Vicar of Wakefield*. New York: New American Library, 1961.

• Higdon, David Leon. "The Critical Fortunes and Misfortunes of Defoe's *Roxana*." *Bucknell Review* 20 (1972):67–82.

• Hume, Robert D. "The Conclusion of Defoe's *Roxana*: Fiasco or Tour de Force?" *Eighteenth-Century Studies* 3 (1970):475–490.

Hunter, J. Paul. *The Reluctant Pilgrim: Defoe's Emblematic Method and Quest for Form in Robinson Crusoe*. Baltimore: Johns Hopkins University Press, 1966.

Iser, Wolfgang. "The Current Situation of Literary Theory: Key Concepts and the Imaginary." *New Literary History* 11 (1979):1–21.

————. *The Implied Reader*. Baltimore: Johns Hopkins University Press, 1974.

• Jackson, Wallace. "*Roxana* and the Development of Defoe's Fiction." *Studies in the Novel* 7 (1975):181–194.

James, Henry. "The Art of Fiction." In *Theory of Fiction: Henry James*. Edited by James E. Miller, Jr. Lincoln: University of Nebraska Press, 1972.

————. Preface to *The Tragic Muse*. In *The Art of the Novel*. New York: Scribner's, 1934.

Johnson, Samuel. *Johnson on Shakespeare*. Edited by Arthur Sherbo. The Yale Edition of the Works of Samuel Johnson. Vols. 7 and 8. New Haven: Yale University Press, 1968.

————. Preface to *A Dictionary of the English Language*. In *Rasselas, Poems, and Selected Prose*. Edited by Bertrand H. Bronson. New York: Holt, Rinehart and Winston, 1952.

————. *The Rambler*. Edited by W. J. Bate and Albrecht B. Strauss. The Yale

Edition of the Works of Samuel Johnson. Vols. 3–5. New Haven: Yale University Press, 1969.

Kermode, Frank. *The Genesis of Secrecy: On the Interpretation of Narrative.* Cambridge and London: Harvard University Press, 1979.

Koonce, H. L. "Moll's Muddle: Defoe's Use of Irony in *Moll Flanders.*" *ELH* 30 (1963):377–394.

Kraft, Quentin. *"Robinson Crusoe* and the Story of the Novel." *College English* 41 (1980):535–548.

Krieger, Murray. "Fiction and Historical Reality: The Hourglass and the Sands of Time." In *Literature and History.* Berkeley and Los Angeles: University of California Press, 1974.

McKillop, Alan D. *The Early Masters of English Fiction.* Lawrence, Kan.: University of Kansas Press, 1956.

Mill, John Stuart. *On Liberty.* Edited by David Spitz. New York: W. W. Norton, 1975.

Moore, John Robert. *A Checklist of the Writings of Daniel Defoe.* 1960. Reprint. Hamden, Ct.: Shoe String Press, 1971.

———. *Daniel Defoe: Citizen of the Modern World.* Chicago: University of Chicago Press, 1958.

Nelson, William. *Fact or Fiction: The Dilemma of the Renaissance Storyteller.* Cambridge: Harvard University Press, 1973.

Nicholson, Watson. *The Historical Sources of Defoe's Journal of the Plague Year.* Boston: Stratfort, 1919.

Novak, Maximillian E. "Crime and Punishment in Defoe's *Roxana.*" *JEGP* 45 (1966):445–465.

———. *Defoe and the Nature of Man.* Oxford: Oxford University Press, 1963.

———. "Defoe's 'Indifferent Monitor': The Complexity of Moll Flanders." *Eighteenth-Century Studies* 3 (1970):351–365.

———. "Defoe's Theory of Fiction." *Studies in Philology* 61 (1964):650–668.

Peckham, Morse. "The Infinitude of Pluralism." *Critical Inquiry* 3 (1977):803–816.

Price, Martin. *To the Palace of Wisdom.* 1964. Reprint. Carbondale, Ill.: Southern Illinois University Press, 1970.

Rader, Ralph W. "Defoe, Richardson, Joyce, and the Concept of Form in the Novel." In *Autobiography, Biography, and the Novel.* Berkeley and Los Angeles: University of California Press, 1973.

———. "Fact, Theory, and Literary Explanation." *Critical Inquiry* 1 (1974):245–272.

———. "Literary Form in Factual Narrative: The Example of Boswell's *Johnson.*"

Works Cited

In *Essays in Eighteenth-Century Biography*. Edited by Philip B. Dahglian. Bloomington, Ind.: Indiana University Press, 1968.

————. "The Literary Theoretical Contribution of Sheldon Sacks." *Critical Inquiry* 6 (1979):183–192.

Richetti, John J. *Defoe's Narratives: Situations and Structures*. Oxford: Clarendon Press, 1975.

Richter, David H. *Fable's End: Completeness and Closure in Rhetorical Fiction*. Chicago: University of Chicago Press, 1974.

Robbe-Grillet, Alain. "A Future for the Novel." In *For a New Novel*. Translated by Richard Howard. New York: Grove Press, 1965.

Rocks, James E. "Camus Reads Defoe: *A Journal of the Plague Year* as a Source of *The Plague*." *Tulane Studies in English* 15 (1967):81–97.

Rogers, Pat, ed. *Defoe: The Critical Heritage*. London: Routledge and Kegan Paul, 1972.

Rousseau, Jean-Jacques. *Émile, ou de l'éducation*. Paris: Garnier Frères, 1961.

Sacks, Sheldon. "*Clarissa* and the Tragic Traditions." In *Irrationalism in the Eighteenth Century*. Edited by Harold E. Pagliaro. Cleveland: Case Western Reserve University Press, 1972.

————. *Fiction and the Shape of Belief*. Berkeley and Los Angeles: University of California Press, 1964.

Scholes, Robert, and Kellogg, Robert. *The Nature of Narrative*. New York: Oxford University Press, 1966.

Schonhorn, Manuel. "Defoe's *Journal of the Plague Year*: Topography and Intention." *Review of English Studies*, n.s. 19 (1968):387–402.

Searle, John R. "The Logical Status of Fictional Discourse." *New Literary History* 6 (1974/5):319–332.

Secord, Arthur W., ed. *Defoe's Review*. Facsimile edition. 22 vols. New York: Columbia University Press, 1938.

————. *Studies in the Narrative Method of Defoe*. 1924. Reprint. New York: Russell and Russell, 1963.

Showalter, English, Jr. *The Evolution of the French Novel, 1641–1782*. Princeton: Princeton University Press, 1972.

Sidney, Sir Philip. *A Defence of Poetry*. Edited by J. A. Van Dorsten. London: Oxford University Press, 1966.

Smollett, Tobias. *Roderick Random*. New York: New American Library, 1964.

Sophocles. *Oedipus the King*. Translated by David Grene. In *The Complete Greek Tragedies*. Edited by David Grene and Richmond Lattimore. 4 vols. Chicago: University of Chicago Press, 1959.

Starr, G. A. *Defoe and Casuistry*. Princeton: Princeton University Press, 1971.

————. *Defoe and Spiritual Autobiography*. Princeton: Princeton University Press, 1965.

Stephen, Leslie. "Defoe's Novels." In *Hours in a Library*. 3 vols. 2nd ed., rev. London: Smith, Elder, and Co., 1892.

Stewart, Philip R. *Imitation and Illusion in the French Memoir-Novel, 1700–1750*. New Haven: Yale University Press, 1969.

Sutherland, James. *Daniel Defoe: A Critical Study*. Cambridge: Harvard University Press, 1971.

————. *Defoe*. Philadelphia and New York: Lippincott, 1938.

Tillyard, E. M. W. *The Epic Strain in the English Novel*. London: Chatto and Windus, 1958.

Todorov, Tzvetan. *The Poetics of Prose*. Translated by Richard Howard. Ithaca, N.Y.: Cornell University Press, 1977.

Trent, William P. *Daniel Defoe: How to Know Him*. Indianapolis, Ind.: Bobbs-Merrill, 1916.

Watt, Ian. *The Rise of the Novel*. Berkeley and Los Angeles: University of California Press, 1957.

Wilson, Rawdon. "The Bright Chimera: Character as a Literary Term." *Critical Inquiry* 5 (1979):725–749.

Wilson, Walter. *Memoirs of the Life and Times of Daniel Defoe*. 3 vols. 1830. Reprint. New York: AMS Press, 1973.

Woolf, Virginia. "Defoe." In *The Common Reader*. New York: Harcourt, Brace and World, 1925.

————. "How It Strikes a Contemporary." In *The Common Reader*. New York: Harcourt, Brace and World, 1925.

————. "Robinson Crusoe." In *The Second Common Reader*. New York: Harcourt, Brace and World, 1932.

Wordsworth, William. *The Prose Works of William Wordsworth*. 3 vols. London: Moxon, 1876.

Zimmerman, Everett. *Defoe and the Novel*. Berkeley and Los Angeles: University of California Press, 1975.

Index